W9-AGD-536

Virtuality Check

Virtuality Check

Power Relations and Alternative Strategies in the Information Society

FRANÇOIS FORTIER

VERSO

London • New York

First published by Verso 2001
© François Fortier 2001
All rights reserved

The moral rights of the author have been asserted

Verso
UK: 6 Meard Street, London W1F 0EG
USA: 180 Varick Street, New York, NY 10014–4606

Verso is the imprint of New Left Books
www.versobooks.com

ISBN 1–85984–628–9

British Library Cataloguing in Publication Data
A catalogue record for this book is available from the British Library

Library of Congress Cataloging-in-Publication Data
A catalog record for this book is available from the Library of Congress

Typeset in Bodoni by M Rules
Printed by Biddles Ltd, Guildford and King's Lynn

Contents

CONTENTS

Acknowledgements

This book is partly based on doctoral research done at York University between 1991 and 1996. For their financial support to the latter, I am grateful to both the Social Sciences and Humanities Research Council (SSHRC) and the International Development Research Centre (IDRC) of Canada. While all responsibility for the following argument, and its omissions, remains my own, my thanks also go to Professor Liisa North for her dedicated support throughout my doctoral work, and to Nils Zurawski, Dominique Caouette, Julian Stallabrass, Sebastian Budgen, and Robin Blackburn for material provided or comments made at different drafting stages of this book. I am also most grateful to Bob Cook and Gillian Beaumont for their patient and meticulous editing, and, especially, to Tran Thi Thu Trang, my wife, for her research and countless contributions to the argument.

I

Introduction

Cyberspace is often glorified as a sword of postmodern enfranch-
isement, promising (once again) liberation from alienating work,
urban dehumanization, corporate greed, and the spectre of
industrial apocalypse. It is said to open the road to a (slaveless
and gender-balanced) Athenian democracy, universal knowledge and wisdom, leapfrogged post-industrial Third World
development, empowered consumerism, and friction-free capitalism.[1] Even more importantly information technologies are
presented as the engine of a third industrial revolution, following mechanization and automation, which, with its computing
power, will lead humanity into the limitless marvels of life sciences, particularly genetic technologies. Others, however, vilify
cyberspace as the latest mirage of bourgeois mystification,
threatening (once again) the working classes with corporate

1

slavery, consumers with mental colonialism, and citizens generally with panoptic totalitarianism.[2] The opening of the genetic Pandora's box, particularly on the terms of profit-seekers, can lead only to the worst possible *Blade Runner* dystopia, with its baggage of extreme inequality, slavery-type exploitation, sanguinary repression, total and final wars, and the eventual demise of biological existence itself. Incipient political and legal battles are already raging between these perspectives, with debates on public access and information monopolies, policies and strategies on proper courses of action, and court cases in the areas of censorship, cryptography, content rating, and privacy.

Yet, floating somewhere between this virtual heaven and hell, the truth about the infosphere remains hard to pin down. Humans are still living in societies with real relations – relations of exploitation and oppression, but also of resistance and solidarity, which lead to the creation of and struggle for alternatives. Much sweeping-away of fantasies, mystification and scarecrows is needed if we are to uncover the foundations, trends, stakes, battles, and consequences of the so-called electronic frontier and its *new economy*. Technologies are neither the naive product of disinterested science nor the deterministic bearers of social processes. They are shaped by existing social relations, while in turn they open up opportunities for social change. This explains how, while information and communication technologies (ICTs) were originally developed by state and corporate sectors, and still largely respond to their needs, other groups have also been able to use such technologies to their own ends. These include civil society organizations, often of progressive and democratic inspiration.

In this book I ask whether information and communication technologies, in their current forms and trends of development, are plausible democratic vectors in relations of both production and reproduction. In order to conduct this analysis, my argument first focuses on current views about the relation between society and technology in general, and information and communication technologies in particular. My purpose is to locate disparate discourses in comparative perspective, and to highlight their divergent representation of socio-technical processes. Beyond intellectual curiosity, an epistemological review is useful for uncovering the links between ideas and the material roots that beget them. Since 'theory is always *for* someone and *for* some purpose',[3] the intention here is ultimately to decipher the political economic assumptions and implications of analytical choices made about ICTs.

I then go on to consider how information and communication technologies are being developed, and how they subsequently affect social relations through their use of and impact on various forms of information, each form being manipulated in different ways through new ICTs, with different political economic implications in each case. If we are to understand these implications, we need to analyse how the technology changes the way we create, capture, store, exchange, compare, modify, own, hide, or destroy various forms of information. In the sphere of production, information takes the form of capital goods and processes, becoming technologies that we value and exchange as industrial patents, such as machines (including ICTs themselves), manufacturing processes, or artificial genomes. By changing the way this information is controlled, ICTs allow valuable knowledge to be relocated from certain groups to others, and to modify the production process. Information can also help the circulation of products, as is the case for trademarks (branding), prices (valuation), and currencies (exchange). Here, ICTs may affect the processes by which products are branded, valued, and exchanged for the conversion of production into profits and, ultimately, the distribution of wealth. Media and entertainment products, in turn, are both commodities (cultural goods and services protected and made profitable by intellectual property rights) and means of social reproduction, as discourses carrying ideological content. For both these functions, media ownership and gatekeeper positions are greatly valued and fought for. In this process, ICTs and digital networking are playing an increasing role, sharpening the tools of discursive construction. Finally, information also serves the transformation or maintenance of social orders by either a more direct (less mediatic) control of information flow (political

4

propaganda, agitation, censorship, and disinformation) or the surveillance of individual behaviour (political beliefs and acts). Here again, ICTs have dramatic implications for the ability of various social groups to control information flow, and ultimately to change the balance of political power.

It is from the perspective of these four processes, two of production (production and trade) and two of reproduction (media and politics), that I consider how ICTs are deliberately designed and used for particular political economic objectives. The presumed opportunities of the so-called information society appear to be less revolutionary than they are claimed to be, for they enhance, but do not transform, the current logic of capitalism – that is, its mechanisms of production and accumulation. In the end, the argument presented here concludes that ICTs, in their current forms and use, are clearly not vectors of democracy. The development of these technologies is steered in the interests of dominant social sectors, enabling new forms of control in production (over labour and consumers) and reproduction (over audiences and citizens), thus further polarizing economic and political power, and threatening many groups with more exploitation and oppression.

Yet my argumentation also points out that ongoing democratic efforts of technology appropriation by civil society organizations do exist, but need to be seen in their wider context, with the overall balance of social implications taken into account. In the last chapter I take a quick glance at these efforts, focusing on the key elements of a strategy for democratic information and communication that could better serve grass-roots emancipation. Some of these initiatives, for lack of political analysis, have assumed that closing the digital divide with an accelerated and expanded deployment of information technologies would suffice to bring the benefits of the latter to everyone. This assumption fails to recognize the role of ICTs in social processes, and how an uncritical adoption of technologies can in fact perpetuate and accentuate exploitation and oppression. I therefore call for alternative appropriation of ICTs, discussing the limits and potential of that strategy but emphasizing the necessary political rather than technical nature of that process and its organic grass-roots ownership. The key points of a strategy that can secure such an ownership, notably the identification of constraints and potential particular to the grass roots, are briefly discussed.

II

Discourse of Machines and
Machines of Discourse

Definitions

Before I go on to the argumentation, in the following paragraphs
I discuss a few key conceptual definitions in order to avoid
confusion or misinterpretation. These definitions make no pre-
tence of being definitive, or even of roughly covering the
debates that concepts often generate. Rather, they seek to provide a common ground for the purpose of the current
discussion. The first of these concepts – already used above –
is that of *information and communication technologies*, which
can be briefly defined, for the purposes of this book, as tools
and processes that permit us to produce, manipulate, and
communicate information. They include computer hardware,
input and output peripherals, storage media, software, and digital communication systems.[1]

Another concept, often more seriously ambiguous, is that of *civil society*, understood here as a space of social relations of reproduction, distinct from both production and formal state activities.[2] Civil society is defined in relational terms – that is to say, not as actors with particular identities but as actors in particular relations with the state and organizations of production. The purpose is to define civil society not as a specific group of organizations but as a range of relations focused on preserving or changing a social order, irrespective of their instigators, separate from the state itself. This approach avoids pigeonholing and imposing artificial distinctions between particular institutions, notably those with overlapping activities. It also defines civil society as a space of relations within itself, between its constituting forces.[3] It is therefore not a unified movement against the state or capital, but a complex structure of conflictive reproduction, intimately linked to production and the state apparatus through the inherent political economy of reproduction itself. The term *grass roots*, in turn, is understood as an intentionally loose group of organizations that emerge from and work in the interests of those social sectors that are both economically subsumed (in relations of production) and politically oppressed (through the existing order of reproduction). The grass roots necessarily operate within civil society and its reproductive relations, but do not cover the entire spectrum of these relations. This inherently political definition of the grass roots draws attention to the very purpose of their activities – that is to say, political emancipation. This definition thus normatively requires that their work be democratic in nature, so it does not encompass social movements that exclude, for example certain groups on the basis of sex, race, religion, sexual preferences, ethnicity, or other individual characteristics.

Finally, another important clarification is that of *political economy*. Defined here in the historical materialist paradigm, political economy is an analysis of the roots, mechanisms, and purposes of power relations, exerted through relations of both production (of valued goods and services) and reproduction (for the maintenance or changing of the social order and its production processes). This implies going beneath the institutional analysis of formalistic political science, while socially qualifying production beyond economics.[4] Political economy is therefore 'constitutive in that it recognizes the limits of causal determination, including the assumption that units of social analysis interact as fully formed wholes and in a linear fashion. Rather, it approaches the social as a set of mutually constitutive processes, acting on one another in various stages of formation and with a direction and impact that can only be comprehended in specific research.'[5] In other words, political economy refuses to view social relations in terms of their presumed functional utility to society; instead it

9

questions that relative utility for all social groups involved in
a relation. It thus analyses power in terms of its implications
for exploitation (the extraction of one group's labour or
resources by another), resistance (the refusal of that extraction) and oppression (the reaction against that refusal). In
this, political economy is necessarily critical, for it reveals
what discourses and non-critical analysis hide or ignore: the
consequences of power relations for *different* social groups.
Furthermore, this approach reflects not only on the various
forms of power, but also on their reproduction, that is, the
discursive construction of their justification or contestation.
Most importantly, then, political economy is not only a paradigm of social analysis, but also an explicit political choice in
favour of democratic alternatives:

> The political economy of communication – like political economy
> in general – has a prescriptive mission. The purpose of its cri-
> tique is to assist the process of social change, both in terms of
> specific media policies within the context of a capitalist political
> economy and in terms of assisting broader social change toward
> a postcapitalist and more democratic society. Consequently, it is
> an aspect of the political economy of communication to study the
> nature of political debates over communication policy and the
> efforts to establish alternative media, as well as to participate in
> them.[6]

Perspectives

A number of theoretical frameworks have been proposed for understanding the relationship between technologies and societies. Some approaches emphasize the autonomy of technology and science as vectors of positive or negative social change. Yet technologies are not only made of the physical aspects of technical artefacts; they are also, and most importantly, processes through which we manipulate matter and symbols. As such, technologies affect and are affected by the way social relations are established, reproduced, and transformed. In order to situate the argument made in this book, the characteristics and methodologies of four analytical groups of theories addressing the links between society and technology are presented here.[7]

Functional neutrality

Technologies are often presumed to move in a way that is independent from social dynamics, with their history, motivation and trajectory being understood in technical terms. They are seen as emerging from the rationalist and productivist marriage of individual creativity and industrial innovation,[8] being functional to an undifferentiated group. In terms of these assumptions, and of the almost universally held modernist values of education, knowledge, communication, and rationality,

11

ICTs imply 'that a world rewired to connect human beings to vast data banks and communications systems would be a progressive step'.[9] This point of view is still very much alive in the international development community, in government bureaucracies, and in parts of civil society.[10]

Yet this perspective has dramatic social consequences. Most technologies are optimistically assumed to be factors of human emancipation, where 'there is no need for serious inquiry into the appropriate design of new institutions or the distribution of rewards and burdens. As long as the economy is growing and the machinery is in good working order, the rest will take care of itself.'[11] Here, questioning the political history of progress, and ICTs as part of it, is not even an issue. The question of technological development is taken out of the present, ideologically hidden in the determinism of the past and the inevitability of the future.[12] Since it is assumed that progress is inescapable and deterministic, humans and their societies have no other choice but to adapt and make the best of their new fate, or pay the cost of inflexibility. At best, it is recognized that the repercussions of some technologies must be studied and contained, owing to their environmental impact or health hazards. Yet such technological assessments remain unashamedly utilitarian, and they have the sole purpose of mediating between economic development and a functionally defined, universalistic, social well-being. In this context, while atomic energy and genetic engineering may raise concerns, ICTs are still granted considerable immunity from even such mild questioning.

In this logic, much of the literature and many of the programmes relative to ICTs are concerned merely with addressing the so-called digital divide, or the exclusion from information systems and content, and the spectre of polarization between the 'information rich' and 'information poor'.[13] The end result, however, is often to call for better connectivity – that is, for a more extensive and more penetrative development of current systems.[14] The quest for improved accessibility then pervades national IT programmes and, in low-income countries, donor-driven development projects of public awareness, business support activities, public infrastructure works, multipurpose community telecentres (MCTs), and so on.

This, however, is short-sighted, for the instrumental approach is still concerned solely with the *use* of technologies as given artefacts. The advent of these technologies is credited to competition, which is assumed to produce, of necessity, the best possible outcome within a functionally defined understanding of human progress. There are two filters through which technologies are presumed to be examined:

> The first is a technical or scientific screen vaguely composed of the work of scientists and engineers who, with their dedication to rationality and efficiency, methodically subject all technological possibilities to careful and objective scrutiny and select only the

best solution to any given problem. . . . The second screen is an
economic filter, composed of two equally vague mechanisms. Upon
successfully completing the technical test, the selected technologies are subjected to the no-nonsense, cost-accounting,
profit-maximizing evaluation of hard-headed, practical businessmen who seek only the most economically viable technologies from
among those deemed technically superior. The 'real world' savvy of
the businessman, we assume, corrects for the excesses of the less
practical scientists and engineers. Finally, since even businessmen
and their managers can make mistakes in judgement, we rely ultimately upon the fail-safe test administered automatically by the
anonymous operation of the self-regulating market, which allows
only the most economically astute businessmen to survive the
rigours of competition and, with them, only the best technologies.[15]

Needless to say, this point of view puts blind faith in the
redeeming ability of technologies, imputing to them a life of
their own and assuming that they are born, grow, serve, age and
die in a socially ahistorical vacuum. Even worse, by desocial-
izing technology this analysis denies the plurality of
technological alternatives, turning agency into object and
development into destiny.

Instrumentalism

An instrumental perspective recognizes that technologies are
implemented through social relations, for better or for worse.

Typically, 'It is human discretion in the application of science and technology which shapes its good and evil effects.'[16] Being 'indifferent to the variety of ends [they] can be employed to achieve', technologies do not bear social relations in and of themselves.[17] For example, computer networks, irrespective of their inherent characteristics, are presumed to be useful either for state and corporate control and marketing, or for human rights activists and community workers in campaigning and grass-roots organizing. In line with this perspective, many researchers and policy-makers pay attention to possible side-effects and negative implications of ICTs, such as the proliferation of child pornography and hate literature, abuses of privacy by unscrupulous marketers, or the presumed neo-imperialist prevalence of Anglo-American content on the Internet. It then suffices to implement regulatory safeguards whenever necessary, to re-establish the appropriate use and expansion of technologies.

However, by ignoring technological *development* as a social and political process, and assuming instead that technologies have inherent virtues, this analysis fails to question the very nature, the processes, and even the implications of the systems it studies. No attention is paid to the criteria by which a technology is said to be valuable, for what purpose and for whom.[18] This obfuscates the agenda of dominant interests that actually determines each and every step of technological life cycles.

Ahistorical inherence

A third perspective sees technologies as *inherently political by nature*, recognizing that not only their use but also their very characteristics have social implications. Solar energy, for example, is said to be inherently democratizing because it enables small-scale power systems for decentralized generation and distribution. Similarly, nuclear reactors are inherently undemocratic, since they require large-scale plants, centralized power grids, and authoritarian controls for the secure handling of radioactive fuel and waste.[19] In this perspective, information and communication technologies are said to have inescapable implications by virtue of their inherent characteristics. This school of thought includes a large number of optimistic technophiles who maintain that ICTs favour democratization because they are accessible, horizontally networked and distributed tools of multidirectional information dissemination. While some see in ICTs a challenge to traditional management structures and an expansion of the Western model of democracy through unrestricted information flow,[20] others anticipate the rise of a new global civil society through participatory, co-operative, non-hierarchical and affordable networking.[21]

This perspective departs from the naive and benevolent simplifications of the approaches examined above. Nevertheless, it makes the historicist claim that technological innovations, in and of themselves, can lead to paradigmatic breakthrough at the level of social relations. In fact, 'dreams of instant liberation from centralized social control have accompanied virtually every important new technological system introduced during the past century and a half'.[22] Even television was celebrated for 'its power to disband armies, to cashier presidents, to create a whole new democratic world – democratic in ways never before imagined, even in America'.[23] The problem with such historicist claims is not that technologies are not important – they are, and they do have 'revolutionary' implications for societies. However, by paying exclusive attention to these implications, this perspective portrays technologies as the very cause of change, rather than exploring the social processes and relations that thrive *behind and under* technological developments. By seeking to explain the implications of technologies in terms of their inherent nature, it reifies them as social forces *sui generis*, anthropomorphically *acting* in accordance with this supposed nature.[24] It thus conceals the historical processes that have led to the formation of this so-called 'nature', and fails to show why certain characteristics of technological artefacts appear in the first place and are nurtured, while others are muzzled or eliminated. Such an approach, being both historicist and ahistorical, still ends up seeing technology as a determinant of society, rather than the reverse.

This is not only a theoretical weakness of this perspective

but most importantly, a political setback for the Left in its resistance and its search for alternatives.[25] If we are fully to understand how technologies reflect social interests, to understand their risks and opportunities, and act accordingly, we must look beyond the happy-talk of the glorious communications revolution. Hidden agendas must be unmasked in order to locate the forces that develop and maintain a technology.[26]

Historical inherence

Analyses of the fourth category seek to understand technologies in terms of their full multidimensional relationship to social processes. Here, technologies are inherently political, but by process rather than by nature. If we are to understand this political process, technologies cannot simply be defined as systems of artefacts, nor merely as 'the type of relationship established between labor and matter in the production process through the intermediation of a given set of means of production enacted by energy and knowledge'.[27] A more complete definition has to encompass productive relations themselves as integral parts of technological processes, looking not only at their technical but also at their institutional and distributional characteristics.[28] This implies 'the preparation, mobilization, and habituation of people for new types of productive activity, the reorientation of the pattern of social investment, the restructuring of social institutions, and, potentially, the redefinition of social relation-ships'.[29] This perspective recognizes technologies as fields of social struggle, driven primarily by the tremendous stakes carried by technological development.[30] In essence, 'science and technology have no character other than the historical and social forces of their creation, application and socialization'.[31]

This definition, with its emphasis on social interests, high-lights the deliberate and systemic nature of technological development. Original ideas and innovations are just one ingre-dient of technological change. The fact that one direction of development becomes dominant:

> is probably less a reflection of its actual technical or economic superiority than of the magnitude of the power which chose it, and of the dominance of the cultural norms which sanction that power. Conversely, if some alternatives have failed to survive, this does not necessarily mean that they were technically or economically in-ferior, but merely that they were deemed inferior according to the criteria of those in power, and thus denied. Once denied, moreover, their futures were further foreclosed by all subsequent investment in the preferred alternative, which rendered any revival of the lost possibility progressively less 'realistic'.[32]

The interests vested in a given form of technology explain the biases in its development, while each form of technology implies a given distribution of its benefits among different social sectors. Powerful groups are thus likely to choose technologies that are not necessarily best suited to so-called *progress*, but most profitable to themselves.[33] Central to technological development is the mutually beneficial relationship between institutions of technological production and those of social power, whereby the means of research and development are provided on condition that they reflect the needs of dominant sectors for economic accumulation and political reproduction.[34] This does not imply that technological development is a grand conspiracy but, rather, that technological artefacts are developed by and come to live among societies, acquiring their characteristics not so much by chance, but more *by design*.[35] This design process includes funding mechanisms for state and corporate research and development (R&D), decisions about investment and production, educational programming, marketing, and managerial choices over agendas for implementation. As dominant sectors have, by definition, more leverage in social struggles, and ultimately over so-called social choices, it comes as no surprise that most technological development primarily reflects the economic interests and political agenda of these groups, while it is self-perpetuating.[36] In what Winner calls a 'régime of instrumentality',[37] technologies are shaped by such constraints, embedding characteristics of domination as technologies take on life, and eventually imposing their not-so-natural logic upon relations of production and reproduction, including further technological development itself. The effects can be lasting: 'After the design has been implemented, the system organized, and the infrastructures put in place, the technology then becomes deterministic, imposing the values and biases built into it.'[38]

Radio, for example, has been deliberately developed for uni-directional broadcasting from central transmitter to receive-only stations: 'The actual structure of radio use embodied centralized economic and political institutions that shaped the technology as a means of building mass audiences for profit and for one-way political discourse.'[39] Yet this development could have led elsewhere – to interactive and bi-directional capabilities.[40] Similarly, organizational groupware packages containing extensive monitoring and surveillance functions are being developed, constraining workflow and communication by means of narrowly defined lines of authority, routing, and screening of information. Here again, the technology could serve less hierarchical purposes, had it not been systematically developed to serve the interests of capital. Another example is that of the micro-browsers needed for wireless mobile networking, which contain built-in functions for user profiling and narrow-casting, notably the automatic identification and geographical localization of the handset. This is rationalized on the basis that small screens compel providers to send only the most appropriate information for each client. Yet this is not inevitable, as better demand-driven search agents and navigational tools could also serve that purpose. Of course, the marketing industry, pursuing its offensive by stealth, is keenly interested in these built-in functions. The alternative would permit consumers to remain anonymous, retaining the ability to make choices at every step of their information search, eventual consumption, or political expression and decisions.

The Internet has indeed raised great hopes of democratization, yet this technology is the product of military and corporate needs for cybernetic intelligence and control. Between the initial ARPANET (Advanced Research Projects Agency Network of the US Department of Defense) funding in the mid-1960s and the completion of the Internet's institutional privatization in April 1995, the network has mostly benefited the United States government, its military apparatus and research institutions.[41] Large-scale corporations have also invested heavily in networking technologies, recognizing, long before the advent of the public cyberspace, the paramount importance of data flows for their industrial, commercial and financial activities. As with other means of communication, data transmission networks are crucial to capitalist accumulation, allowing improvements in research and development, assisting design and manufacturing, adjusting markets, and helping with the reduction of stocks, the transfer of funds, the trading of commodities and – as noted above – the control of labour. Networking also increases the mobility of corporations, further consolidating their power in relation to states and civil societies in the areas of taxation,[42] labour and environmental regulations, and other conditions of investment. Not surprisingly, this has opened opportunities for what Castells calls the *global criminal economy*.[43] Most crucially, financial operations have been greatly improved by computer networking, 'unifying capital, markets, and leading to 24-hour "follow the sun" trading'.[44] For over two decades, international financial operations have relied on specialized agencies, such as Reuters' international money market service or the Society for World-wide Interbank Financial Transactions (SWIFT), which provide speedy and secure transactions.[45] As early as 1981, the transnational data flows of American Express Corporation reached approximately US$10 billion a day.[46] Similarly, financial transactions on the world's major stock exchanges are vitally dependent on computerized data flows, within and between themselves. At the London, New York, and Tokyo exchanges, transactions in the currency market alone were reaching US$623 billion dollars per day in 1992,[47] and 1.5 trillion globally by 1998.[48] In all, financial institutions are responsible for about 80 percent of global data communication.[49] 'By allowing round-the-clock capital investment opportunities worldwide, internationalization dramatically increases the rate of turnover of capital, thus enhancing profit levels for a given profit rate.'[50] Computer networking thus serves to reduce delays and contract space to accelerate the production, circulation and realization of capital – a velocity which, in turn, crucially conditions the creation, extraction, and accumulation of surplus.[51] Even when small-scale telematics appeared in the late 1970s, it was primarily for commercial purposes, with expensive (up to US$200 per hour) online financial and professional database services. These included Datalog, The Source, and Compuserve, controlled by corporations such as IBM, Sears, H&R Block, and Lockheed.[52] Now, as in its infancy, computer networking caters for those who can invest in its research and development, or purchase the technology once it has been commercialized.

This perspective on ICTs underlines the point that information is power, but not in and of itself. It is power only to the extent that it is grounded in material reality – that it has consequences for how people act, and thus for how societies produce value and reproduce relations of order and change. Historical materialism will remain relevant to the analysis of the information society for as long as 'virtuality' is real. Taking the fourth theoretical perspective presented here, the argument below shows that information and communication technologies – and computer networking in particular – largely reflect both the economic interests and the political agenda of dominant sectors, leaving little room for naive technophilia and calling for great caution in planning alternative use of ICTs. Dedicated infrastructures and commercial services provide capital owners and other dominant sectors with a tremendous economic and political advantage over labour and other contesting movements within civil society. The question raised here on ICT development is therefore not about its unintended consequences but about the intended – if not always explicit and open – purposes of the technology. In other words, this approach does not fear technology for what is unknown but, rather, seeks to warn about technology for what is actually known, but often hidden, and should be brought to light. This is what this political economy of the information society is proposing to do.

III

Information Society or Control Society?

Subsuming Labour: Cybernetic Productivity

Many people have claimed that since the late 1960s, global capitalism has entered a post-industrial phase. Manuel Castells argues that while industrial knowledge was crucial to the development of the means of production during the previous era, *knowledge-processing knowledge* is now the engine of this development, shifting the immediate object of production from the maximizing of output (under industrialism) to the *accumulation of knowledge* as a means of maximizing output (under informationalism).[1] This characterizes a post-Fordist capitalist *mode of development*[2] which he calls the *informational society*.

For Castells, productivity in this new regime is 'based on

enhanced ability to store, retrieve, and analyse information, [where] every single discovery, as well as every application, can be related to developments in other fields and in other applications, by continuous interactions through the common medium of information systems'.[3] This is brought about by the unique characteristics of information and communication technologies that produce and transform information: 'What computers do is to organize the sets of instructions required for the handling of information, and, increasingly, for the generation of new information, on the basis of the combination and interaction of stored information.'[4] In this context, information and communication technologies are seen as the new key factors of productivity and competitiveness, through innovation and flexibility.

From this perspective, the full potential of ICTs is reached through a synergetic networking and interaction of research and production, which is possible only in 'an atmosphere of freedom'.[5] Castells cites the example of the Soviet Union, which refused to facilitate such democratic information flows by limiting the spread of information technologies within its civil society. He argues that 'without this diffusion, information technologies could not develop beyond the specific, functional assignments received from the state, thus making impossible the process of spontaneous innovation by use and networked interaction which characterizes the information technology paradigm'.[6] Therefore – according to Castells – while ICTs can enhance productivity, they require democratic systems that liberate information flows and permit free knowledge-processing to flourish. If capitalism needs the increased productivity, it therefore has no choice but to accept the full democratization.

This analysis, however, remains questionable on a number of points. First, growth and economic development do not necessarily need democracy (at least, not beyond a narrowly defined utilitarian version of it), as many fast-growing newly industrialized countries have shown. In various forms, capitalism systematically needs an ability to exploit and oppress, if only to maintain profitability in the face of increasing competition, both domestically and internationally. Difficulties in doing so have contributed to the contradictions that catalysed the crisis of Fordism in the late 1960s. They have been the single most important target of the neo-liberal politics of the so-called flexible accumulation over the last thirty years,[7] characterized by accentuated surplus extraction, economic polarization, and more intense political control[8] wherever ideological hegemony lost ground. So it is theoretically problematic to argue that, through the information revolution, capital would barter democratization for productivity.

Second, the qualitative implications of ICTs have to be weighed against the procedural, organizational and political constraints on information and knowledge-handling. A profound breakthrough in *knowledge-processing knowledge*, as described by Castells, would require that information be free and accessible in a process of open networking, collegial information-sharing, and co-operative work. This is exemplified by the co-operative development of Open Source Software such as the Linux operating system, essentially based on a gift rather than a profit economy.[9] In turn, co-operative research conducted under the umbrella of the Human Genome Project has been led by public funding, well beyond the usual competition of the free market.

Both cases are certainly not typical of the greater part of capitalist production. More commonly, the processing of knowledge is industrial, often intra-firm and bureaucratic, and network security remains a constant obsession of corporations and state apparatuses, superseding connectivity itself. Most information and knowledge are valued, and treated accordingly with price tags, intellectual property rights and recognition (such as academic citation), patents, security, secrecy, hoarding, manipulation, or sabotage. Better tools for transforming and communicating information certainly improve knowledge-processing activities, but willingness to share or conceal information remains a separate issue. Indeed, Microsoft's concerns about Open Source Software development illustrate the way free networking is feared by corporate interests.[10] The myth of open networking reverts naively to the age-old encyclopaedic dream of a 'world brain', already envisaged in the 1930s, in which 'a wealth of knowledge and suggestions – systematically ordered and generally disseminated – would probably . . . suffice to solve all the mighty difficulties of our age'.[11]

Since it is clear that ICTs do not – most of the time – enhance co-operation, Castells's argument on productivity, based on such co-operation, remains ambiguous. There is in fact an ongoing debate about the 'computer productivity paradox', which addresses the overall impact of ICTs on output and the apparently small returns these technologies have brought, despite engulfing half of all capital investments over recent years.[12] It was only in 1995, after at least fifteen years of significant capital investment in new information technologies, that productivity figures started rising beyond 1.5 per cent a year in the United States. Yet, as some studies are now revealing, the impact of ICTs on labour productivity may still be fairly limited beyond the computer hardware industry itself and the telecommunications, automotive and steel-making industries: that is, roughly only 12 per cent of the United States economy.[13] These reservations stem from recognizing the part that cyclical factors play in current productivity figures, and take into consideration the new accounting methodology adopted by the US Commerce Department, which now treats software as investment rather than expenditure.[14] Furthermore, in the computer hardware sector, manufacturing processes and changes in products themselves (notably the exponential increase in the density of integrated circuits and the corresponding computing power) may explain higher output per worker in larger proportion than the actual use of ICTs.

On the other hand, Castells's analysis of productivity is problematic also because it considers ICTs solely in terms of their impact on processes of production. It assumes that productivity, usually defined as output per person-hour, increases with the use of ICTs through automation, and new forms and organization of production which respond better to supply and demand.[15] These include flexible specialization, just-in-time manufacturing and stock management, total quality, precise execution, decentralized production and management, horizontal, networked, and virtual corporate structures, telework, flexi-time, global finances, and – the mother of all realization – friction-free capitalism. In fact, however, these forms of production organization are also the techno-managerial component of a capitalist strategy to make its workforce more 'flexible', and increase control over processes of production.

This highlights the fact that a simple definition of productivity as output per person-hour does not permit a complete analysis of why output may increase. The definition remains silent on the multiplicity of processes by which additional output can be extracted from labour in a given time, for it indiscriminately bundles together skills, know-how, tools, and processes, but also incentives and means of coercion. In other words, when productivity statistics increase, this may be owing to any combination of the above factors, including the possibility of little improvement in tools but many new ways of coercing labour. This distinction has important implications for the way the impact of information technologies on the production process is analysed, as it refocuses attention from labour productivity alone to the broader issue of relations of production.

All this raises doubts about whether productivity gains are really the main motivation behind the development of ICTs. There may be a number of reasons why entrepreneurs invest in information technologies. In neo-classical economics, investment decisions are based on relative factor analysis, where opportunity costs are rationally scrutinized. In practice, however, this is a questionable assumption, as other factors must be taken into consideration. These may include the enthusiasm of management for new technologies, an ideology of progress, the efficient marketing of machine and computer manufacturers who nurture this ideology, or the more prosaic tax deductions available on capital investment.[16] Decisions may also be motivated by the hoarding behaviour of managers worried about losing opportunities (as with new markets available only through electronic commerce), or missing out on changing production paradigms (as with ICT-led automation). Furthermore, the interrelationship between information technologies and production processes or organizational structures may change over time. While ICTs may be introduced for some specific purpose, and with the expectation of given changes, the actual result may be somewhat different. This is due in part to unexpected characteristics of the technology, but also to the dynamic imposition and resistance encountered in changing relations of production. All these possible motivations, and their dynamic over time, need to be explored further, and put into balance and perspective of their particular circumstances.

Thus a number of assumptions need to be questioned in the rather universal belief that links incentive, innovation, productivity, competitiveness and prosperity, for each of these steps does not necessarily lead to the next. If it does, in turn, it might be through relations of power and undisclosed motivations that require critical analysis.[17] This is not to say that innovations, in information technologies as elsewhere, have had no or little impact on productivity. The ambiguity of the process and its unclear implications, however, should warn us that there might be a great deal that still needs to be uncovered. In any case – and while the continuing debate goes beyond the scope of this book – the uncertainty of the impact of ICTs on productivity supports the separate argument that the development of and massive investment in ICTs are also serving another, maybe more important purpose, beyond the mere search for ever-increasing productivity. Investment decisions are therefore most probably also motivated by relations of production, which remain barely analysed, or euphemistically referred to as workers' flexibility and discipline, or 'labour-market rigidities', in much of the literature.

At the very heart of the so-called information revolution is *cybernetic control*, which gave birth to ICTs and promoted computer networking as a tool of communication and remote interaction. The term *cybernetics* was coined from the Greek word for *steering* or *control*,[18] implying the perception of reality, the differentiation of this reality from a normative ideal, and an action or a feedback to modify reality accordingly.[19] Unlike previous tools and forms of automation, information technologies are said to be general in their application, and flexible in their ability to control their environment cybernetically – in a way, similar to humans themselves. As a result, they are *meta-technologies* of control over other activities and technological processes at all levels of production and reproduction.[20]

Through ICTs, 'human expertise has been congealed into software, making it an object that can be possessed by others'.[21] David Noble has shown that managers chose digitally controlled machine tools not because of their productivity – they were in fact less efficient than analogue record playback machines – but because digital technology allowed managers to further subjugate skilled machinists and increase supervision of the shop floor through centralized programming.[22]

> Where people were once generally central to the industrial and bureaucratic process and able to leverage their share of its benefits, now machines and machine intelligence are central. Where hand tools and machines requiring attentive, intelligent, and even skilled workers to operate them, had been the means of production in the industrial era, cybernetic systems and intelligent communications networks have taken over, and these systems require fewer people – and less of their intelligence and involvement.[23]

Based on a legitimizing discourse of efficiency,[24] cybernetic automation allows management to consolidate its control over production processes not only through the appropriation of knowledge, but also through vastly improved monitoring and restriction of information flows.[25] These practices in turn permit management to delocalize and fragmentize production, so that it can benefit from variable costs of factors of production, and ultimately increase profitability. To this end, it will deskill labour, dismantle unions, prevent other forms of solidarity, spatially individualize workers in isolated units or locally bound subcontracting companies subsumed to global competition, and – in the end – 'discipline' the workforce.[26] From the point of view of many trade unionists, this is by no means a novelty of capitalism, as it has been pervasive since the Industrial Revolution:

> The developing consciousness of the Australian trade unionists
> illustrates the old challenge of the Luddites to the factory-owners:
> 'you haven't any right to take over my tools and skills and build
> them into a machine [that] you, alone, own and whose products
> you, alone, sell in the marketplace.' This old objection is being
> resurrected again as owners of technology and capital build the
> skills, experience, and knowledge of millions of office and factory
> workers into the micro-machine process that make them
> unemployed.[27]

With the exception of a privileged minority of highly skilled
workers, ICTs have brought little emancipation to most of the
workforce: 'For what looks like a growing majority, it is not
knowledge that the new economy wants, but dexterity: manual
dexterity and mental dexterity to adjust to new operating systems and cope with the pace involved.'[28] Shop-floor control has
been largely enhanced through the design of machines that are
said to be 'idiot-proof' by limiting workers' intervention to a
minimum. Needless to say, this 'engineering mentality betrays
a rather cynical view of human beings (not to mention an elitist
and derisive view of subordinates) in which any chance for
human intervention (by workers) is negatively assumed to be a
chance for error rather than, more positively, a chance for
creativity, judgement, or enhancement'.[29]

Moreover – and often beyond the constitutional and legal
protection of state–civil society relations – the workplace is
frequently subject to pervasive hierarchical surveillance and

monitoring, unabashed in its violation of workers' privacy, all in the sacrosanct name of efficiency and ownership prerogatives.[30] This is technically permitted by what Philip Agre conceptualizes in the capture model, founded on socio-technical processes of digitizing and accumulating sequences of events related to given activities. This capture of data, through automated sensors or recorded human actions (e.g. the swiping of a magnetic card), allows objects and humans to be tracked on request, while building up statistical databases of such activities. Agre points out that 'capture is never purely technical but always *sociotechnical* in nature. If a capture system 'works' then what is working is a larger sociopolitical structure, not just a technical system.'[31]

In fact, 'It would be extraordinary if a technology as rich in opportunity for extending control as office automation were not seized upon to exploit this aspect of its potential, even at the cost of some loss of productivity.'[32] And corporations do indeed perceive cybernetic technologies, and new ICTs among them, as an opportunity for intensifying automated surveillance through remote cameras, tracking devices, and broad activity recording. 'Software exists to allow employers to screen employees' electronic mail (for example, to pick up a word such as "résumé" or "cv"), and such screening is legal in most countries. Network servers also allow employers to monitor, record, and censor the sites employees are visiting.'[33] In support of these technological options, British corporations are lobbying the government to 'secure the right to read employees' e-mails when workers are off sick or on holiday'.[34]

> A study of 1,085 firms concluded by the American Management Association in 1998 showed, for example, that 40% of them are engaged in some form of intrusive surveillance of their employees. They read electronic mail, monitor telephone conversation, examine the content of voice mailboxes, log the passwords of personal computers, record work performance on digital video.[35]

The current deployment of network computers consolidates these control functions. In fact, organizational hierarchies have little to fear from information technologies. If ranks and channels of authority have survived the telephone and casual conversations in lifts, they will survive electronic mail. It is power relations – not some intrinsic character of paper – that have determined the workflow embedded, for example, in office memoranda.[36] The same is true of the workflow routing now offered with most groupware packages, safely programmed and with characteristics kept far beyond the workers' level of access. Furthermore, the expanding practice of teleworking, besides the benefits it may represent to some professionals, enables new forms of surplus-labour extraction, since it is increasingly muddled up with the private sphere of the household. In a rerun of the putting-out systems of the Industrial Revolution, rental and utility costs are partly or wholly transferred to employees, contracts are made precarious, labour time may be increased, and family labour may be put to contribution without compensation.[37]

In the end, all the above practices permit new contractual arrangements to reduce workers' power in production relations, and increase capital owners' ability to reduce labour costs, extracting further surplus-value, often in absolute terms. While other, more traditional methods of labour discipline have also been used by capitalist states for the last twenty years, the place of ICTs in such class struggles has undoubtedly been central. This is well demonstrated by the 1981 US air traffic controller labour dispute:

> Perhaps the most dramatic example of the power that owning software gives management over professional employees possessing formerly vital skills comes from the 1981 strike by U.S. air traffic controllers. In preparing for contract bargaining with the Professional Air Traffic Controllers Association (PATCO), the Federal Aviation Administration (FAA) secretly developed automated 'flow control' systems that could take over tasks of regulating aircraft movement. The system played a critical role in allowing the Reagan administration to fire 12,000 controllers and still maintain acceptable air service with substantially fewer personnel. The strike was broken and the union decertified.[38]

Since then, trends in technological development have contributed to make many jobs in the new economy insecure and badly paid, sometimes supplemented with shares whose values are volatile, if not speculative. Staff turnover in call centres, for example, is typically between 50 and 70 per cent.[39]

The argument above is not intended to fuel some conspiratorial paranoia of technological development, or of managerial obsessions with labour control. In practice, the deployment and use of ICTs have led to various information systems, with a broad range of power relations and implications for workers.[40] Yet there are discernible trends in the way ICTs have affected relations of production. Beyond the productivity debate, what the analysis reveals is a drastic displacement of wealth from labour to capital in a systematic neo-liberal restructuring, enabled in part by ICTs engineered specifically for this purpose. This could explain – at least in some measure – why capital owners have persistently invested huge sums in the deployment of such technologies, irrespective of the actual gains in labour productivity achieved through the use of ICTs. They may often have done so not only (if at all in some cases) to increase labour productivity, but to secure managerial control of the labour process, and for the consequent expropriation of wealth in their own favour. By focusing on productivity, the discourse of the information revolution has overlooked the implications of ICTs for relations of production and reproduction, notably control of accumulation.

This conceals the sectoral interests such technologies represent and the contradictions they necessarily beget, or affect, between labour and capital. The argument made above thus proposes that far from revolutionizing the way capitalist societies produce, ICTs actually contribute to the realignment of the *distribution* of that production among various social groups.

Trapping Consumers: No Free Cyber-Lunch

From the military, scientific, geek, or even techno-anarchist preserve it used to be, the Internet has now clearly been turned into a virtual marketplace for serious business, even a whole 'new economy'. With the privatization of its infrastructure and processes in the early 1990s, the pipes of the Internet are now controlled by – among others – MCI-Worldcom, IBM, Network Solutions, AT&T, and General Atomics.[41] These corporations have acquired the legal rights to profit from managing the network, including its resource allocation, protocols, addresses and domain names, access, indexes and tariffs, and will no doubt act accordingly.

> The most pressing question for the future of the Internet is not how the technology will change, but how the process of change and evolution itself will be managed. . . . The architecture of the Internet has always been driven by a core group of designers, but

the form of that group has changed as the number of interested parties has grown. With the success of the Internet has come a proliferation of stakeholders – stakeholders now with an economic as well as an intellectual investment in the network. We now see, in the debates over control of the domain name space and the form of the next generation IP addresses, a struggle to find the next social structure that will guide the Internet in the future.[42]

In principle, Internet standards are discussed and adopted by institutions with open memberships: the Internet Engineering Task Force (IETF) for the development of technical standards, the Steering Group (IESG) for their implementation, and the Internet Corporation for Assigned Names and Numbers (ICANN) for the supervision of the domain name system. In practice, one of the bodies that weighs heavily in these decisions is the World Wide Web Consortium (W3C), whose membership is largely composed of over 400 companies which pay annual dues of $50,000.[43] To judge from the latest decisions on the creation of new top-level domain names at the March 2000 ICANN meeting in Cairo, the overwhelming power of these corporate interests has already defined the 'next social structure' of the Internet.[44] These trademarked corporations, as information property owners, have successfully lobbied to slow the growth in the number of new top-level domains, thus protecting their own private interests: 'They have invested a lot of money in their names and have often fought or bought off 'cybersquatters', people who register web addresses merely to sell them later. New domains risk diluting these brands and might also increase the costs of policing them.'[45]

The very growth of commercial Universal Resource Locators (URLs) over the last six years is highly revealing about the commodification of the Internet. By July 1994, between 12,000 and 18,000 organizations had already requested registration of a commercial domain name from Network Solutions (one of the corporations now administering the Internet). A year later, the number had increased to between 60,000 and 80,000, and was close to 300,000 by July 1996.[46] Three and a half years later, at the end of 1999, there were nearly 7.2 million registered dot-com domain names – that is, four times as many as the dot-net and dot-org domains combined.[47] This shows to what extent commercial interests now largely dominate the Internet.

And the stakes of such development are enormous. As in many infant industries, online traders still suffer from an insatiable need for capital. To take only the most notorious: Amazon.com has been losing colossal sums of money: $120 million in 1998, and $250 million a quarter in 1999.[48] But these hormone-grown dot-coms are unlikely to remain in the red for much longer. Whether the speculative stock market bubble bursts or not for Amazon and the like, capital has poured in on the assumption that there will be handsome long-term dividends once such companies have established themselves as the few surviving branded e-commerce retailers: 'In 1999, global e-commerce was worth a little over $150 billion. Around 80% of those transactions were between one business and another. Yet growth of all forms of e-commerce is hectic. Business-to-business web exchanges are mushrooming. In America e-retailing revenues tripled last year; in Europe and Japan they rose faster still.' [49] While retail e-commerce remains small (less than 1 per cent of retail trade in the USA, and ten times less than current catalogue trading), it is expected to grow quickly. In some sectors this share is already much higher – 15 per cent of retail stockbrokerage and 5 per cent of book sales.[50] By 2003–04, business-to-consumer online trading could reach $184 billion, while business-to-business could reach $3 trillion. Within a few years, this could represent 5 per cent of retailing in the United States, and could be up to 15 or 20 per cent by 2010.[51]

Some of the e-commerce frenzy is a new disguise for old tricks, simply offering a faster and more convenient search and ordering process than was previously offered by catalogue and phone retailers. But with recent web technologies, commerce has also developed in new directions. One need only think, in the sphere of business-to-business e-commerce, of electronic integration in production, circulation, and cycle-wide feedback mechanisms. In consumer e-commerce, the key point of interest on the supply side is in new forms of data mining for profiled marketing.[52] E-trading naturally applies to dematerialized digital products such as software, copyrighted texts, MP3 music, travel arrangements, and banking operations. However, other types of goods and services – from books, CDs and fast-food restaurants to grocery, drugs, and art works – are also being channelled swiftly in realspace thanks to newly established delivery infrastructures and distribution symbioses between e-traders and a few established retailing franchises.

In the most refined liberal tradition, this is all trumpeted as the consummation of perfect trading, the friction-free capitalism of – at last – fully sovereign consumers. The Internet and online trading are said to empower consumers by allowing them to compare prices at a click of the mouse, to share experiences about product quality through electronic discussion forums, to make better deals through bulk purchases, and to respond to global discount auctions and classifieds of all sorts.[53] This is said to create:

> an economy that is close to the theoretical models of capitalism imagined by Adam Smith and his admirers. Those models assumed that the world was made up of rational individuals who were able to pursue their economic interests in the light of perfect information and relatively free from government and geographical obstacles. Geography is becoming less of a constraint; governments are

becoming less interventionist; and information is more easily and
rapidly available.[54]

Studies have indeed shown that:

> online retailers tend to be cheaper than conventional rivals, and
> that they adjust prices more finely and more often. But they also
> find that price dispersion (the spread between the highest and
> lowest prices) is often as wide on the Internet as it is in the shop-
> ping mall – or even wider. Moreover, the retailers with the keenest
> prices rarely have the biggest sales.[55]

But if investors were flocking to e-commerce stocks in the way
they were, it could not be for fear of a consumer empowerment
that would threaten traders, producers, and, ultimately, profits.
On the contrary, capital owners are expecting huge rewards –
partly from taking trade from other merchants, and partly from
consumers' pockets. Far from believing in consumer sovereignty, their assumption is that 'customers will align themselves
early on with one of a couple of names and stay put out of sloth
and habit'.[56] And to make sure that consumers, whether sloth-
ful or not, stay put, the marketing industry is developing tools of
unprecedented potential. For one thing, consumer-driven comparison price search engines are likely to be discredited by
commercial disinformation, from anonymous marketers if
need be. The most reliable reviews will thus remain those
available through more credible professional sources such as

specialized publications and consumer associations. Offline, a multitude of rewards systems, from supermarket point cards to airline miles, have long sought the faithfulness of consumers by increasing the opportunity cost of moving to new suppliers. Online, new loyalty programmes and 'one-click shopping' customization, dependent on recurrent visits and purchases, are being implemented through the same principle, increasing allegiance and discouraging customers from shopping around.

But most importantly, online at least as much as offline, trademark branding has been central to consumption behaviour. The branding process enables consumers to recognize and trust products, either for their quality (BMW, Lloyds) or for their connotation (Coke, Pepsi).[57] Online, trade and product brands can thus address – at least in part – security concerns about the delivery and quality of goods and services, as well as the confidentiality of transactions and the safety of payment which is most often done using credit cards. And it has been found that 'even people who use "shopbots", or computer programs that search many websites for the best deal, usually buy from the market leader – even if it is not quoting the lowest prices'.[58] An online executive puts it cynically: 'Coca-Cola doesn't win the taste test and Microsoft is not the best operating system, but in America brands win.'[59] For the sake of branding, the advertising disbursement of online retailers through web portals or traditional media is enormous – already in 1998 an estimated $100 million for Amazon.com alone.[60] This seems to be bearing fruit: 'Rather than rooting out the cheapest deal, most consumers go directly to Amazon.com or Cdnow, even though, the research shows, they charge 7–12% more on average than such lesser-known retailers as Books.com and CD Universe.'[61] It shows that branding is not losing any of its traditional importance online, and that the Internet mostly reproduces existing practices of market domination.

Profiled marketing

Despite having the potential to empower consumers through enhanced information flows, the new ICTs are in fact serving commercial interests by greatly reinforcing marketing practices. While such practices long preceded electronic commerce, ICTs now allow merchants to perfect online *profiled marketing*. By monitoring and recording every possible behaviour of online consumers – such as personal data, online navigational habits, interests and preferences, and responses to given situations – online marketers can conduct data mining that produces individual records or statistical aggregates. They can then use these data to categorize consumer classes or perform personalized marketing, known as narrow-casting.[62]

The marketing industry often presents consumer profiling

and narrow-casting as tools of convenience, allowing traders to respond better to consumer needs and tastes, and tailor offers to specific client characteristics. This is said to spare consumers from bombardment with unsolicited information through burdened web pages or junk mail. From the consumer's point of view, these tools undeniably present certain benefits.

It is naive, however, to surrender the selection of content to commercial providers, for they will necessarily take advantage of that control of supply to influence consumer choices. Narrow-casting allows e-traders to benefit from improved marketing, but also to prevent access to competing information through the filtering of content, all in the name of consumers' own preferences. This also permits manufacturers and traders to channel demand towards the most profitable goods and services, and to ensure the stability of demand, and therefore income. Thus, despite purporting to be demand-driven, narrow-casting actually proposes a supply-driven approach to information. While conventional mass-media marketing sought to foster conformity of consumption and its moulding to the requirements of production, narrow-casting continues to manipulate wants and demand, but now enables this supply-driven mass-production process to lie hidden behind tailored permutations of more of the same with different bells and whistles. The technique renders online comparison of prices and quality ever more impractical, for the products appear increasingly differentiated, albeit superficially. In addition, profiling permits online retailers to estimate, from previous behaviour, how much a consumer may be willing to pay for a given product. The price offered through narrow-casting can then be adjusted to the highest acceptable point for each customer.[63] Profiling and narrow-casting may actually reduce the transaction costs of many commercial exchanges, making them more predictable and decreasing overheads for both demand and supply activities.[64] Yet by also allowing manipulation of information and demand itself, and increasing monopolization of transactions, the process distorts market exchanges for the benefit of monopolistic suppliers.

While it is true that digital automation of assembly lines may allow flexibility in production, this does not guarantee the 'acceptance of variety' as forms of 'different social and cultural subsystems'.[65] In fact – and much more insidiously – the use of ICTs in profiling enables 'a new set of techniques by which the search for information about individuals and the delivery of homogenizing socialization messages can be performed in a variety of ways for a variety of segments of society'.[66] The marketing industry has quickly recognized the significance of such tools, since they translate into enormous profits for traders who attract and retain consumers. The astonishing valuation of Amazon.com, at its current assessment (or even at a quarter of it, assuming the further bursting of that bubble), is based in part upon its ever-growing data mines.[67] The fact that three companies bankrupted in the spring of 2000 – Boo.com, Toysmart and CraftShop.com – succeeded in selling or were trying to sell private consumer information such as credit card numbers, addresses and consuming patterns gives additional evidence of the value of data mines. Liquidations never pay much, but 'Customer lists are considered among the most valued assets of any technology company'.[68] This is also confirmed by the case of America Online, which has records of over 21 million subscribers, including personal data and detailed navigation habits between news, e-mails, chat rooms, databases and other services within its proprietary system: 'That trove of data could bring huge revenue if AOL were to package it for sale to retailers, banks, insurers and others dying to know which AOL customers would be most likely to snap up their products and services.'[69] This potential is increased immensely by AOL's merger with Time-Warner, which has databases for the 'reading and listening habits of the 65 million households that receive its books, magazines and CDs'.[70] Many other online providers, notably those that grant free Internet access, are known to collect navigational data and use it for their own profiled marketing, or resell it to advertising firms. In such a process, merchants better control information flows and manipulate the spending of the not-so-sovereign consumer.

This consolidation of existing social segmentation can follow both commercial and political behaviour, whatever the purpose of a given campaign, and whenever the marginal benefit of homogenized mass propaganda begins to decline.[71] All this takes consumers further away from their supposed demand-driven sovereignty. The political economic implications of profiling and narrow-casting, in class formation and other processes of social differentiation, are significant:

> the capacity to socialize different portions of society into different values, attitudes, and lifestyles, and to do so from one generation to the next, seems to offer considerable stability to market segmentation as a technique for the rationalization of consumption. This means that the demassification of society may actually be a powerful reinforcement of social stratifications that could be hereditary and, because they would work through individual motivation, self-enforcing.[72]

Data mining, profiling and narrow-casting, as forms of automated customer relationship management, bring a new dimension to relations of production in the sphere of circulation or, in a similar process, in relations of reproduction in the sphere of ideology. They enable commercial or political propagandists to establish even more unequal relations between them and the object of profiling, based on the unilateral accumulation of knowledge by such organizations over individuals.

Monopolization of trade

Beyond increasing the direct control of merchants over consumers, electronic commerce may also bring about the concentration of the entire trading industry. In the process of acquiring and keeping an ever-larger number of consumers, online retailers are building e-commerce oligopolies while threatening many small retailers, both on- and offline.

On the one hand, the largest manufacturing corporations – notably in the auto, garment, and agri-business sectors – are already assembling huge consortiums for business-to-business electronic trading, creating powerful monopsonies.[73] Other sectors – such as banking, finance, and stockbroking in particular – will also undergo dramatic restructuring through mergers and closures, for their services are inherently subject to online trading. Retail banking operations, for example, are nine-tenths less expensive online than in branches, and half as expensive as through automatic telling machines.[74] This threatens the survival of small unbranded banks, while labour throughout the industry has already suffered severe layoffs.

On the other hand, it is expected, if not already confirmed, that up to four-fifths of today's Internet start-ups will not survive for long, and will either be bought off by the big players or forced into bankruptcy:

> Unlike today, where an explosion of technology companies compete
> for venture capital, experts predict the Internet economy of 2005
> will be a network of established businesses whose influence comes
> from and stretches around the world. And it will be full of old-world
> names that many investors have been ignoring – behemoths such as
> Procter & Gamble, Chevron, Coca-Cola and Boise Cascade.

In the end, there will be a few companies dominating guarded domains, with only 'three or four giant portals, three or four giant e-tailers, three or four giant Internet service providers'.[75]

Already, 'nearly three-quarters of Internet-related initial public offerings in America since mid-1995 now trade below their issue prices'.[76] Following the bursting of many e-trader stocks in 1999 (often by 90 per cent of their peak valuation), a spate of closures, layoffs and mergers has begun.[77] Launching an e-business was a cottage industry five years ago (as was Jeff Bezos's Amazon.com), but there will henceforth be very few new entrants. The cost of a viable start-up in e-commerce is already estimated to be around $50 million to $100 million and rising, while investors are now shying away from a market they have found to be saturated.[78]

As we have seen, electronic commerce is still in its infancy, with a limited share of overall trade. But once e-commerce has absorbed even a small share of overall retailing activities, this may threaten many offline merchants, particularly those with slim profit margins and those – mostly small-scale traders –

who are dependent on trademarks they do not control.[79] This will make them vulnerable to online competition from large-scale branded distributors and manufacturers. It is expected that by 2003, 18 per cent of book retailing in the United States will be done online, yet a drop of only 15 per cent may make the business unprofitable for many shops, forcing them to close.[80] It will be worse still for travel agencies, whose 'margins are so thin that a loss of only 3–5% of the market to the Internet threatens to drive large numbers of traditional travel agents out of business'.[81] But the share of e-commerce in travel retail had already reached 2 per cent by 1999, and is expected to rise to 12 per cent by 2003.[82] Similarly, the average stock market value of local and regional newspapers has already decreased, as investors expect publishers to lose much of their classified advertising revenue.[83] Some capitalists are themselves concerned: 'Andy Grove, the head of Intel, has told congressmen that the "Internet is about to wipe out entire sections of the economy – and has warned them that, unless politicians start moving at "Internet rather than Washington speed", America may see a repeat of the social disaster that followed the mechanisation of agriculture.'[84]

Yet another technology that may soon greatly contribute to commercial concentration is the convergence of wireless telephony with the Internet. Already on the market, Wireless Application Protocol (WAP) systems enable many new services to be provided on cellular handsets by Internet marketers, including the sale of digital audio broadcasting and MP3 music formats. Furthermore, over the next three years a number of new mobile telephone systems will be introduced, allowing broadband data transmission (of up to 2 megabits per second) for handheld wireless devices. These will accommodate a range of computer applications, including standard e-mail, Internet browsing, and even video streaming. The mobile phone and other wireless terminals will thus become key interfaces for accessing the Internet, and therefore to conduct lucrative e-commerce. By 2004 there will be more than one billion mobile phones, twice as many as the number of personal computers.

The political economic implications of these forthcoming developments in cyberspace may be seen in the improved profiling of consumers and more efficient access to them. WAP providers claim that the micro-browser terminals, by virtue of their smallness, compel them to profile clients better, enabling only the most relevant data to be sent.[85] But the technology itself also permits very specific narrow-casting, thanks to the precise knowledge that providers have about handset owners, including their detailed identities, current locations, calendaring preferences, and so on.[86] This will also be true of other future wireless access technologies.

In turn, the new terminals are giving mobile telephone

providers the opportunity to replace Microsoft's ubiquitous Windows operating system with their own 'desktops', and the channels and links that clients need to access the Internet. Controlling this access ultimately means controlling the way clients purchase, and this is the key to the so-called new economy. Once again, stock market behaviour reveals much about the phenomenon. The value of mobile phone providers is now to be found in what access to clients they can leverage, and investors are certainly expecting huge returns from current strategic positioning. Early in 2000, Vodafone AirTouch paid $180 billion for the purchase of Mannesmann – that is, nearly $12,000 for each of the 14 million Mannesmann subscribers.[87] Furthermore, in spring and summer 2000 the European auctions of radio frequencies for third-generation mobile telephony, totalling $36 billion in the United Kingdom and $45 billion in Germany, showed the willingness of established companies to protect their foothold in a lucrative market, but also the high returns expected from mobile Internet services.

Enthusiasts say that information and communication technologies revolutionize trading by submitting producers to laws of demand. Yet ICTs, in their current form of development, enable the fragmentation of consumers through profiled marketing and unprecedented levels of supply-driven manipulation of wants, further accelerating the current restructuring and monopolization of trade. This has the consequences of reducing consumer choice over brands, shops, and the purchasing process, while threatening the imposition of monopolistic prices – all for the empowerment of traders, not of consumers, in a form of *friction-free corporatism*.

Influencing Audiences:
The Cyber-Manufacturing of Consent

It is true – and crucial to this argument – that progressive sectors of civil society have been able to make alternative use of the new technology, and to carve inroads into the corporate cybernetic agenda. From 1982 to the early 1990s, the adoption of computer networking by several civil society organizations opened a window of opportunity.[88] One key achievement has been the creation and refinement of many-to-many interactive networking tools, which are often mistakenly understood as being inherent to the technology rather than developmental choices and initiatives. This is particularly true of the widespread deployment of electronic fora (newsgroups and mailing lists) and low-cost connectivity through numerous bulletin board systems, Usenet, and Fido networks. Without such technical appropriation, and left to the vagaries of marketed supply, computer networking might now be much less interactive and participatory. The window of opportunity materialized in the form of networks such as Peacenet, the Web, Alternex, and other members of the Association for Progressive Communication (APC), as well as independent organizations such as Britain's Poptel, Italy's Agorá, and numerous bulletin board systems worldwide. They have allowed much information to circulate among activists, and have given birth to affordable alternative online news services, from a handful in the 1980s to several thousand today. The prompt and strategic development of these services gave them a conspicuous role at the dawn of cyberspace, and offered an encouraging indication of how the political future of the technology might have developed.

Computer networking suffers few constraints of time, space and volume, with relatively small marginal costs, at least for institutional users. It is indisputable that the technology can significantly improve the exchange of logistical information within and between organizations, and increase access to documentation and dissemination of produced information. The political implications of the technology would then reside 'in its capacity to challenge the existing political hierarchy's monopoly on powerful communications media, and perhaps thus revitalize citizen-based democracy'.[89] But these hypothetical implications must be seen in the social reality in which they operate. Is this use of technology *actually improving the overall balance of power* in favour of the grass roots? The answer depends not on how the technology is used by any one sector, but by all of them. The generalized use of computer networking simply moves 'the baseline that defines electronic dimensions of social influence. [Thus,] Using a personal computer makes one no more powerful vis-à-vis, say, the National Security Agency than flying a hang glider establishes a person as a match for the U.S. Air Force.'[90] To flag circumstantial uses without putting them in the context of a wider set of relations is necessarily misleading. If it is true, for example, that computer networking provides quick and cheap communication for human rights activists across continents, it grants the same resource to neo-fascist rock bands for the broadcasting of hate songs – and much greater resources to well-endowed corporations and states. In the end, who – between Amnesty International and the white supremacists of Resistance Inc. – will get more out of cyber-networking and broadcasting?

The mobilization against, and successful derailing of, the Multilateral Agreement on Investment (MAI) and the Seattle Millennium Round of the World Trade Organization are other examples of how the Internet is said to revolutionize civil society politics, short-circuiting mainstream media and permitting cheap and instantaneous grass-roots logistics worldwide. An activist noted that 'the immediacy of the Internet has changed the dynamics of advocacy campaigns'.[91] This argument, however, misses the greater picture of ICTs, which also changed the dynamics of capitalism. Globalization itself, and the new international regimes sought by multinational corporations under the MAI and Millennium Round, would not even be an issue without ICTs.[92] Computer networking may help activists to resist, but it also – and much more significantly – permits globalization in the first place. To say that the Internet will democratize politics is the same as arguing that the steam locomotive revolutionized labour relations by allowing trade unions to organize, while forgetting that the new engine was a key vector of industrial capitalism in the first place. The sole potential of computer networking tells us precious little about its social implications. Most importantly, it says nothing of the ability of progressive sectors to organize and mobilize social movements, to invest resources and time, to take risks and forgo opportunities in order to engage in political struggles that affect existing social relations. Resistance to the MAI is imputable to civil society activism, *not* to computers. There was life, including networked activism, long before the Internet, and sometimes in much more vivacious and spirited forms than today.[93]

Even when access to information is improved, this serves a purpose only where both demand and supply can diversify: 'What is missing in most accounts of the "information society" is an understanding of the way in which knowledge and information mediate relations of power.'[94] Since the emergence of mass-media politics, lack of access to information has not been the main obstacle: 'information is for the most part already available, and if power remains centralized, it is because information itself is never enough'.[95] The idea that access to information is democratizing 'mistakes sheer supply of information with an educated ability to gain knowledge and act effectively based on that knowledge'.[96] With its current trends, cyberspace does little to increase 'educated abilities', let alone critical ones. A political economy less indulgent than the enthusiasm of some cyber-activists shows that while anyone may publish almost anything which millions may download, little attention is ever paid to independent unbranded sources of information. Unlike earlier civil society developments in electronic networking, the recent explosion of the Internet in its World Wide Web applications owes a lot to its glossy commercialization and market profitability, and relatively little to socially motivated activism.

Behind the infrastructure corporations are the media and software giants freed, over the last decade, by digital convergence and deregulation of media cross-ownership in the United States and elsewhere. There has already been a formidable process of media concentration, starting with traditional media corporations such as Time-Warner and Disney-ABC Capital Cities taking over theme parks, television channels, and cable distributors. The next step has been for 'old media' such as

Time-Warner and Seagram to merge with 'new media', respectively America Online and Vivendi. In the process, Microsoft, Silicon Graphics, Tele-Communications Inc., and Sun Microsystems have come in with colossal capital investments, lining up to provide content and to link the Internet with television broadcasting and wireless telephony.[97] These mergers and cross-ownerships provide the survivors with the means to control both the technology, which they can more easily develop for their specific requirements, and the content, which they own and distribute themselves. The stakes of this new 'winner-takes-all' rule are enormous, reflecting the magnitude of market hegemony. Epitomizing the process, the Star Wars trilogy has generated over four billion dollars in revenues from box offices, videos, CD-ROMs, toys, video games, books, clothes and other accessories.[98]

Many independent initiatives continue to foster grass-roots communication and information exchange. But as the market race for commodified information is unleashed, the dice will henceforth be heavily loaded in favour of well-endowed corporate players. For example, Internet service providers 'are moving toward an ability-to-pay pricing structure and shunning periodicals that do not bring in large revenues, especially politically progressive publications that are not in vogue or do not have sufficiently large subscription bases'.[99] As a result, alternative information providers are today swimming in rough seas filled by hungry sharks such as CNN Interactive, USA Today, MSNBC, and *The Financial Times*. All large North American and European media organizations – including 700 newspapers already by early 1997[100] – have Web pages, many with round-the-clock updates. Furthermore, the advent (force-fed since Windows 98) of push technologies and so-called 'active channels' compels a pace that only large media organizations can keep up with. In turn, search robots, used on the Internet to locate information, are now renting out keywords at high prices to route users – insidiously, to the highest-bidding client sites.[101] Indeed, the monopolization of Internet navigation has already started: 'tracking of Web sites has shown that 35% of all surfing time is spent on just 50 sites. The research shows that only a handful of sites are capturing an increasing amount of "eyeball" time.'[102] Needless to say, the grass roots and anything on the fringe of commercial mainstream are not going to shine, if they appear at all, on the road maps of the information highway and the Yellow Pages of cyber-emporium.[103] Models are being developed to represent the ongoing geographic and other types of stratification in the visibility on the Internet, whereby a core takes shape around interlinked sites while peripheries remain populated by isolated sites, with little or no connection inward or outward to the core.[104] For many years now, the trend has clearly been towards a uni-directional, top–down, one-to-many medium, with entertainment on demand and pseudo-interactivity.[105] As with other mass-communication technologies, the purpose is to make profits by boosting and reproducing consumerism.

Moreover, this fortified homogenization of discourse serves a propaganda system whose power 'lies in its ability to mobilize an elite consensus, to give the appearance of democratic consent, and to create enough confusion, misunderstanding, and apathy in the general population to allow elite programs to go forward'.[106] In this context, the window of opportunity for civil society is now closing tight, and the so-called electronic frontier is being reordered. Cyberspace is colonized by information brokers, adapting mainstream media structures and practices to online services for government and corporate sponsors. Old wine is poured into new bottles: state and corporate media, entertainment, telecommunication and advertising magnates develop well-branded,[107] user-friendly, attractive multimedia online services with a massive marketing make-up that lures consumers away from a new breed of cyber-marginals – among them precisely those progressive sources that were prominent on the Internet back in the brave new world of the mid- and late 1980s. While the technology exists, at fairly low cost, to provide even television programmes on the Web, branding will be crucial in enticing audiences to tune on given URLs.[108] As the commensurate visibility of marginal providers is dramatically reduced, non-consensual 'noise' on the Internet is as constricted as it has been in the traditional media, and weakened by dominant or consensual cultural parameters.[109] The progressive edge of computer networking – at least on the broadcasting front – is already largely eroded.

As if ideological excommunication was not enough, the accessibility, decentralization, and multidirectional aspects of computer networking could very well be smelted out of the technology. Massive commercial dumping (such as junk e-mailing) and multiplication of resources create acute information overflow. This seriously affects the ability of individuals and institutions to manage and absorb information,[110] resulting in a saturation of information that provides further rationale, for service providers and many users alike, to tame the Internet's anarchy and co-opt it in the realm of legal, ordered civility. Many users, burdened by commercial and ideological bombardments, security hazards, and sluggish connectivity due to backbone saturation, are willing to isolate themselves from the greater Internet. Instead they install or accept screening systems and the selection of messages and virtual fora, thus forgoing not only the practice but even the principle of universal connectivity. Networks thus become increasingly restrictive in both the access to and diffusion of content.

But corporations, by their complicity in such inequality, have been developing networking technologies that serve this purpose for more than a decade. Many companies having 'spent large sums on building private networks which already do everything ISDN is capable of, some of the most sophisticated users do not want a standardized network. For them, having more advanced telecom is a way of gaining a competitive edge.'[111] As Rupert Murdoch crudely puts it: 'Monopoly is a terrible thing until you have it.'[112] Privileged access and 'a competitive edge' are being increasingly secured through the differentiation of service providers: 'Corporate users are demanding improved reliability and performance, and are willing to pay for it. [National service providers] are already experimenting with offering multiple classes of service with guaranteed performance, using a new routing protocol . . .'.[113] On the information marketplace: 'Users will get what they pay for – even if they have to pay a lot.'[114] This is exemplified by Reuters' high-end Internet-like network, running in parallel to the Internet, for its clients in the finance sector.[115] This implies that those who cannot pay will not get much, or that what they do get will be of little value. It will probably result in service stratification of a cyberspace with expensive – but guaranteed – reliable, fast, encrypted, unmonitored and uncensored networks for corporations, states, and the wealthy; and cheaper but unreliable, sluggish, wiretapped, monitored and censored services for others.

Furthermore, the open Internet is also being partially kept in or replaced by proprietary environments, such as the 'walled garden' of America Online, where users remain for about 85 per cent of the time they spend online. This nurtured oasis of consumer services is now blooming with the media fruits of Time-Warner, following the merger of the two giants.[116] Other value-added services, such as Internet telephony, explicitly attempt to keep consumers within the walls for as long as possible – not only for the direct revenues this generates, but also in order to keep control of the lucrative online marketing channels. Microsoft is also bidding for its enclosed pasture through Windows DNA (Distributed interNet Architecture), which provides client–server integration dependent on Windows 2000 or more compact versions of its operating systems (for wireless and other consumer devices).

The rise of the Networked Computer (NC), promoted by a number of industry leaders, is yet another example of the way technological design can further constrain users of information technologies for the benefit of dominant groups. The conventional PC is a combination of hardware and software that provides 'a flexible platform for exploring a wide range of different applications from word processing and accounting to image and audio processing'.[117] Possessing no disk storage, and with a minimal operating system and processing capacity, the NC is confined to user interfaces, leaving the data and applications on a central server linked by data networks. Besides reducing the costs of such appliances (admittedly of much interest to many users), and simplifying the work of system maintenance, this technology also strips users of their autonomy, enabling central management and control over the applications that can run, and making information content ever more vulnerable.

Even more worrying, however, is the fact that merchants never go conquering without soldiers at their flanks. Ostracism outside the mainstream is not the only peril faced by those who, in cyberspace, challenge the dominant discourse. For example, new technologies of commercial network monitoring have 'the added benefit of enabling traffic metering: [National service providers] will know who is sending what packets where, and can charge accordingly.'[118] So, for that matter, will a new breed of lawmakers and cybercops.

Watching Citizens:
Cybernetic Technologies Indeed

It has been argued that the very characteristics of computer networking are rendering the control of the technology, and censorship or monitoring of its information content, difficult to operate and sustain.[119] This, in itself, would supposedly erode the ability of states and corporations to preserve a monopoly on discourse, and to restrict civil society linkages:

Politics and government will be transformed by free communications, changing the balance of power between governments and their citizens. People will become better informed and will be able to communicate their views to their government's leaders and representatives more easily. Politicians will become more sensitive to lobbying and to public-opinion polls, especially in the established democracies. People who live under dictatorial regimes will find it easier to communicate with the rest of the world.[120]

Computer networking also allegedly shifts power from institutions and organizations to individuals,[121] enlarges freedom of the press, and breaks workplace hierarchies, so that information may circulate freely irrespective of rank and status.[122] It has even been argued that with electronic means of delivery, 'the leverage of owning printing plants will disappear. Even having a dedicated staff of reporters worldwide will lose some of its significance as talented free-lance writers discover an electronic venue directly into your home'.[123] Computer networking, with its mailing lists, websites, and even the principle of hypertext itself,[124] is said to bring disproportionate benefits to democratic but media-deprived civil society, with large numbers of participants and scattered resources, rather than to a few powerful monopolies with centralized decision-making. Some even dream of a thriving push-button referendum democracy,[125] believing that the mere availability of information will devolve power to the many.

But as the dust settles on the hype of cyberspace, we can see that the benefits of computer networks can barely maintain the former positions of civil society organizations, let alone emancipate work, empower consumers, or democratize the media. Unless one suffers from conspiratorial paranoia, it is arguable that the Internet has not – yet – become a tool of panoptic control. However, through the now closed window of opportunity, the sky looks increasingly sombre. First, civil rights are under severe attack through the disclosure of private information. This includes, for example, the 'sharing of medical records between health care centers and insurance companies, government interagency record swapping of citizen data, and the selling of driver license data by state motor vehicle registration agencies'.[126] But the capturing of private information also goes much further, notably with legal and illegal police registries that simply disregard privacy as a suspicious luxury. Yet:

> Privacy is not a treasure to be hidden or unearthed. It is a decision to show mutual respect, an arbitrary affirmation of the limits of other people's actions. It is created only by political will underpinning the law. This is the only way personal privacy has any reality, and to forget it opens the door to the most pointless gold rush, whether it feeds on innocent victims or cloaks itself in morality, no longer attacking aggressors for their actions but for their supposed 'secret intentions', making all citizens suspect.[127]

Second, while merchants are cleansing and enclosing the common pastures of cyberspace, liberal democracies and authoritarian regimes alike are taking measures to prevent computer networking from breaching their control over information and ideology. It is true that in the first decade of cyberspace, a series of events took many governments and police authorities by surprise. Through the Internet, expatriate Chinese students mobilized quickly following the 1989 Tien An Men massacre;[128] reformists bypassed the reactionary information blackout during the 1990 Soviet coup;[129] and the *Ejercito Zapatista de Liberación Nacional* brought its version of the 1994 confrontation with the Mexican army straight into press and living-rooms worldwide.[130] But after their temporary dizzy spell, the authorities are now acutely aware of the alternative uses that have been made of new telecommunications technologies. Many are already implementing a wide range of policies and technical measures for subjugating cyberspace or, better still, turning it into a tool serving their own propaganda. This translates into policies that either limit access to computer networking or control the content and flow of information circulating through it. These include regulations on the import, export, manufacture and use of networking equipment, restrictions on the operation of Internet service providers, monitoring of private communications, censorship of public content, and limitations on the gathering, storage, manipulation, and exchange of information.

Through digital networks, wiretapping of all types of communication is made much easier. Being digital throughout, computer-mediated communication is easier to regulate and monitor than analogue voice, printed, or facsimile messages. An increasing number of commercial and social transactions are now leaving digital footprints, easily traceable by corporate and state organizations. Digital text can be automatically scanned, even on a global scale, for keywords and syntax. It can be recorded, logged, screened, sorted, classified, and indexed by origins and recipients.[131] Beyond screening, breaching attempts can be recorded for prosecution. The mere knowledge that such recording takes place is, in itself, a significant deterrent.[132] In the end, while Internet censorship remains permeable and requires continuous monitoring by the authorities, it still succeeds in keeping the vast majority of users in line. Furthermore, automated wiretapping of the Internet and other digital media can easily be used for industrial espionage. Firewalls set up by Internet service providers or national gateways can easily be used to intercept and search all correspondence for commercially valuable information, such as bidding quotations or marketing strategies.

Among the tools of such digital control is *censorware* – that is, software to be mounted on personal computers, servers, and even national gateways, to allow digital screening and monitoring. With such information gates, only normatively defined 'legitimate' information is allowed to go through filters and reach users. There are already several examples of restrictive or prescriptive practices, through filtered browsers, so-called secured gateways, or cleansed sub-cyberspaces. In the United States, content-sensitive firewalls have long been enacted against coarse language and commercial mass-mailing on America Online, Compuserve, Prodigy, and numerous bulletin board systems.[133] Recently, the first 'family-friendly' search robot was made available, automatically blanking-out vast numbers of existing sources.[134] To permit voluntary or imposed screening, the information technology industry – including Netscape and Microsoft in their respective browsers, that is, 90 per cent of the market – has now adopted the Platform for Internet Content Selection standard (PICS). Other filters based on keywords, URLs and rating are also spreading rapidly, and many search robots are planning to disregard unrated sites.[135] The Federal and State governments are currently trying to impose the use of censorware in schools and public libraries; this would prevent access to a large number of sites from public facilities.[136] Beyond the United States, filters have already been put in place by state-controlled gateways in many countries, notably China, Iran, Saudi Arabia, and Vietnam.[137] Since 1996, Singapore's oligopolistic Internet service providers are imposing , for private users, the routing of connections through censored proxy servers.[138] In Israel, Toranet allows access only to kosher-certified Internet sites.[139]

Censorware renders invisible a large proportion of the material on the Internet, blocking not only what is judged morally or politically questionable by authorities or service providers, but also untargeted material. The search robot cited above that offers a 'family-friendly Internet' has been found to filter 90 to 99 per cent of otherwise available material.[140] Even when intended for end-user parental control, censorware remains 'clumsy and blocks out a whole range of legitimate non-obscene speech':[141]

> For example, a site which lists the contact information for groups of lesbians and gay men interested in square dancing is blocked by many of the filtering software makers, who are either unable or unwilling to consider that information about sexual orientation and identity has nothing to do with sexual behavior, and everything to do with culture and identity.[142]

Other casualties include scientific information containing sexually or anatomically explicit language; sites advising on safer-sex practices, contraception, abortion, or several forms of cancers, and HIV-AIDS; and resources for victims and prevention of rape or human rights abuses. Beyond moral sanctioning, the political economic implications of the censorware technology is just a step away:

> The major commercial sites will still be readily available, they will have the resources and inclination to self-rate, and third-party

rating services will be inclined to give them acceptable ratings. People who disseminate quirky and idiosyncratic speech, create individual home pages, or post to controversial news groups, will be among the first Internet users blocked by filters and made invisible by the search engines. Controversial speech will still exist, but will only be visible to those with the tools and know-how to penetrate the dense smokescreen of industry 'self-regulation'.[143]

Of course, filters are never so tight as to prevent reasonably versed users from bypassing secure gateways or accessing marginalized information sources. But the vast majority of users remain under control, while every hacking incident leads to new, more sophisticated security. With these streamlining tools, so long cyberspace, welcome cyber-fiefdom. Filters on networks can then be mounted according to commercial, regional, professional, educational, ethnic, linguistic, religious, racial, gender and class requirements. All this is done ostensibly for respectable and rational reasons – for the sake of accessibility if not intellectual property, national security, or correct morality. And as with other communication technologies today, a few state and corporate media are to be the gatekeepers of that legitimacy and selection, in authoritarian societies and liberal ones alike. In Rheingold's words, they will seize the Internet, 'censor it, meter it, and sell it back to us'.[144]

Countries like China and Vietnam have recognized the contradiction between their eagerness to liberalize information and electronic transactions of a business nature, and their obsession with maintaining control over other information flows both within their country and with the outside world. This led a Vietnamese official to state, rather metaphorically, that his country welcomes the fresh air the Internet window offers, but needs to prevent flies from coming in at the same time. Such a contradiction is to be addressed by adopting a series of technical measures and policies that will provide the necessary space for business-related information and communication, while stiffly monitoring and restricting content of any other social and political character. Similarly, Chinese officials have expressed their willingness to let business networks develop, as long as they keep off politics: 'They view that as the benefit and the (reason) for providing access and would shut anything down that does not meet that criteria.' Obviously wary of their market share, ISPs are inclined to play by the rules and focus on lucrative commercial clients, steering clear of serving the potentially problematic broader public. Compuserve is unequivocal: 'In China, we aim for the high end . . . so that censorship issues will not be as big a problem.'[145]

Besides technical means of control, dominant economic and political actors are calling for regulations that permit the curbing of cyberspace's alleged moral or political abuses and the prosecution of offending users, service providers, or common carriers.[146] While Iraq and Myanmar, among several other

77

countries, practically forbid Internet access, the United Arab Emirates and China compel holders of electronic accounts to register with police authorities.[147] In Vietnam, to avoid the anonymous sending of messages, the government had, for a long time, forbidden the use of public e-mail accounts in cyber-cafés. Illegal and so-called problematic content is being addressed by a number of legislatures worldwide.[148] For example, the United States Federal and State governments have taken several initiatives to prevent certain information and technologies circulating freely on the Internet. The US Supreme Court has now repealed the 1996 Communication Decency Act, but a range of fresh regulations is now being presented.

Many people, of all political allegiances, rejoice at the checking of dystopian or criminal activities in cyberspace, most notoriously child pornography, hate literature, and the piracy of intellectual property. Much media and policy attention is given to them, but also to more benign forms of deviance from con-formity, and for dubious purposes that go beyond the public interest: restrictions and surveillance in these grey areas also conveniently lay the ground for more politically motivated controls.[149] In the name of national security, the White House, and the departments of Justice and Defence, have long been attempting to restrict cryptographic technologies, which allow ordinary users to secure their communications with highly robust password-protected encoding. Through the now defunct

Clipper Chip project and more recent initiatives, the authorities have tried to enforce either weak or key-escrow cryptographic systems that they can easily scrutinize. It is obvious that drug and arms dealers, paedophiles, terrorists, and spies would not obey anti-cryptographic laws that impose the use of weak algorithms or third-party key-escrow services. Such laws thus probably owe more to the demand of police authorities and security agencies, which wish to maintain their historical not-so-judicial ability to monitor the wider population.[150] In 1999, the Internet Engineering Task Force (IETF), one of the network's regulatory bodies, was discussing the embedding of wiretapping facilities into the Internet standards.[151] This was rejected for the time being, but it certainly bears witness to the prevailing tensions and possible technological developments already pushed on several fronts by governmental authorities, in the United States as elsewhere.

Across the Atlantic, a French official watchdog organization estimates that over 100,000 illegal wiretaps are conducted annually, while 'There have been numerous cases in the United Kingdom which revealed that the British intelligence services monitor social activists, labor unions and civil liberties organizations.'[152] In fact, France criminalized civilian cryptography altogether between 1990 and 1996, and maintained severe restrictions for a few years thereafter,[153] more fully liberalizing its use only in 2000. The OECD, for its part, has established recommendations for common rules, which open the way to 'lawful' but unspecified 'access to plaintext, or cryptographic keys, of encrypted data'.[154] In fact, the British Regulation of Investigatory Powers Act (RIPA), effective from October 2000, allows government agencies to monitor Internet communication. This includes 'the ability of the police and others to demand the release of "keys" (ranging from simple passwords to complicated encryption techniques) to electronically encrypted material. The law gives the Home Secretary an ominous-sounding power to require the installation of interception devices (known as "black boxes") by Internet services providers (ISPs).'[155] The evolution of the cryptographic debate indicates that state security agencies were significantly concerned with their ability to monitor civilian communications. At this stage, it would be speculative to discuss the capacity of these agencies to decipher current levels of civilian cryptographic coding, but the recent British regulation indicates that this does not prevent them from wanting to monitor Internet traffic. Such an ability would certainly at least partly explain the relaxing of legal constraints on cryptography. It is also noticeable that concessions were made only under much pressure from powerful economic interests, themselves preoccupied by the key role of cryptography in the development of electronic commerce.

In short, it is true that computer networking holds significant potential for alternative publishing and broadcasting, and improved logistical communication for the progressive sectors of civil society. Some go so far as to claim that 'the death of distance will shift power downward, to the individual. It will both reinforce democracy and transform it.'[156] But such enthusiasm encourages subjugation through passive gizmo-contemplation. As I argued above, the technology is unlikely to develop spontaneously in these directions, while the medium is quickly being co-opted by the dominant sectors for their own agenda. Apart from significant but rare cases of alternative appropriation, computer networking reflects existing power relations. It is unrealistic to expect that networking will democratize politics simply because the technology *could* be developed for and used to that end. ICTs are, in fact, devout servants of corporate and state control in surveillance, monitoring and policing activities, and in the bureaucratic functions of social services, taxation, immigration, and intelligence.[157]

The stakes are obviously tremendous. Left exposed to neo-liberal logic, cyberspace could open the way to a dreadful cocktail of disinformation and panoptic surveillance, allowing the most consummate forms of interiorized exploitation and oppression. Already, a market-driven and price-tagged pay-toll information highway is materializing, serving those with the highest purchasing power and reinforcing the current structures of domination. Meanwhile, state and corporate apparatuses are closely monitoring network activity for intelligence and propaganda purposes, controlling both content and medium whenever necessary. For all the early enthusiasm, computer networking, in its current forms, is definitely not an almighty weapon of political resistance and counter-formation.

IV

Alternative Strategies

In this chapter I provide a quick overview and critique of existing strategies adopted by a number of agencies for the deployment of information technologies among various social groups. While I do not offer a comprehensive study, I explore alternative strategies by drawing from the experience of activists and progressive developers, and the political economic constraints and potential of ICTs as examined above.

The mainstream strategies implemented by the international development sector have often stressed the importance of bridging the gap between the 'haves' and 'haves-nots' of information and knowledge, against a widening *digital divide*. They seek to address the exclusion of certain groups, social sectors or entire nations, which are left behind the so-called Information Revolution. The problem is examined sociologically, as the result of economic marginalization, or internationally, as a North–South disparity. In either case, it calls for the rich (dominant sectors, the North) to include and *empower* the poor (the excluded, the South), who risk further impoverishment if they stand by while the *new economy* is taking shape. Strategists then seek improved and universal accessibility through national information technology programmes and donor-driven development projects of public awareness, business support activities, infrastructural works, large-scale information technology training, capacity building in local content development, and so on.

This kind of strategy often materializes – mostly in the Third World – into projects that sponsor public facilities such as commercial Internet cafés or multipurpose community telecentres (MCTs), with special attention to the presumed needs of grassroots sectors. Yet the conceptualization and deployment of telecentres often misread or bypass the actual needs of the alleged beneficiaries, and address priorities that are not necessarily theirs. The bulk of the information content provided through exogenously planned and managed telecentres may not fit the actual needs of the grass roots, because they are unable to recognize those needs. For example, a telecentre project officer once commented that since landless peasants do not have land to irrigate, or crops to which to apply extension advice, or poor communities do not have sufficient capital to deploy micro-generators, they therefore have no need for such information in the first place. From the officer's angle, there was thus no point in trying to cater to the needs of the poorest sectors, since the technology had little to offer them, and they were better off with traditional social assistance programmes. In other words, the poor are said to have inadequate resources to make proper use of ICTs; whereas in fact we should recognize that existing information systems provide inadequate content, through inadequate tools, for the poor, and see how this can be corrected. Furthermore, MCTs are mostly located in town centres, and are therefore not likely to reach the most disadvantaged population, who are often illiterate, geographically isolated, stereotypically excluded from fashionable innovations such as telecentres, and too poor to pay for online research or training fees.

With this kind of approach, which merely provides access to new information technologies without questioning their forms and content, these efforts mostly consolidate social inequalities.[1] Despite the best of intentions of much developmental work, projects are still geared towards the needs of dominant sectors, and are thus unlikely to be of much help to subsumed ones. This puts blind faith in an age-old trickle-down fantasy, and can end up being quite detrimental. With their extensive potential for control, ICTs can easily be used to further subjugate these deprived social groups to already existing mechanisms of exploitation and oppression, perhaps even to greater extent than any other technologies in the past. For example, ICTs and telecentres may permit further penetration of central bureaucratic institutions in remote rural areas; these may be used to enforce the collection of taxes, emigration control, or property rights that are beneficial to the landed class, rather than providing services or legal protection for subsistence peasants. The technology can also serve the increased penetration of dubious publicity for commercial agriculture, which often seeks to make farmers dependent on industrial inputs and oligopolistic commercialization. Furthermore, with the current requirement of ICTs for capital investment, skills, and access to infrastructures, and the emphasis of their deployment, they overwhelmingly address the needs of agribusiness firms, with little attention to small and only partially commercialized producers.[2] Growth in the former sector increases pressure on resources held by the latter, notably land and water, while it changes patterns of cultivation and the use of agricultural technologies. So, this type of strategy not only neglects the information needs of small farmers, but also accelerates their insertion into economic processes that they do not control, making it likely that this will be done on terms that are detrimental to them. In such a context, generalized access to information and communication systems mostly serves the reproduction of dominant social relations, at the expense of labouring classes – a bridging of the digital divide with the chains of submission.

Domination and repression never occur in a social vacuum. Attempts by dominant sectors to direct the development of ICTs and their use for control necessarily beget, to varying degrees, resistance and new forms of social conflict. Despite their grim reality, technologies therefore remain what societies make of them, and this necessarily leaves room for resistance and alternatives. ICTs are sites of struggle, 'where the disempowered can take advantage of momentary weakness or inconsistencies on the part of the hegemonic projects. At these times, on specific terrains, people may be able to re-interpret cultural processes and appropriate communications functions to deploy altered meanings and develop oppositional positions.'[3] Once political economic analyses have explained *why* some technological options have been retained and others marginalized, the strategic question then becomes: '*How* could any such alternatives be reclaimed?'[4]

The argument made here does not call for more jumping on to the information bandwagon by merely seeking ever-greater access to and integration in the information society. Rather, the analysis calls for resistance against forms this process and its technologies currently take, and a search for and promotion of alternatives based on a progressive redefinition of what communication and information technologies *should* do. Instead of using ICTs in their current forms, and hoping that this will suffice to democratize information flows, progressive networking must therefore emphasize the appropriation and redesigning of such technologies. As I said above, this has been the strategy of many progressive developers and ISPs for well over a decade, serving civil society with cheap and open fora that better match the specific needs and political objectives of the grass roots. This has shown that resistance and efforts towards alternative development can partly reshape ICTs better to assist progressive movements.

Yet David Noble, studying the case of manufacturing automation, rightly warns us of the risk of being overenthusiastic about the possibilities of appropriating technologies that were designed in the first place for purposes other than democratic ones. From the understanding that technologies emerge amid a political economic process, one can go on to reject them at the outset for necessarily being controlled by dominant interests, and face the unavoidable charges of Luddism and its associated ostracism. Alternatively, one can take on the challenge and political commitment of technological appropriation. However:

> This more optimistic interpretation has generated a great deal of enthusiasm about possibilities and led to a fetish for and fantasies about alternatives. . . . This new, expansive view of technology offered hope of transcending the mere defensive posture of labour. Rather than reacting endlessly, off balance, to management's

technological agenda, labour could now go on the offensive itself by formulating its own alternative technological agenda.[5]

Noble then points out that such an interpretation overlooks the fact that technological development and deployment occurred over two centuries, with characteristics deeply embedded in systems and artefacts – to such an extent that it would take 'years of reflection, research, and practical experimentation',[6] even assuming the resources were available, to come up with alternatives. In the meantime, new technologies are continuously being deployed by and for dominant sectors, only making resistance all the more difficult and prospects of appropriation more remote. He then indicates that the early-nineteenth-century Luddites did at least manage to buy time for workers on the fringe of starvation, but through intense class struggles that are unimaginable in the current era of liberal supremacy and weak labour unions:

> In short, having overcome the ideology of technological determinism, the fatalism of the past, [the appeal for alternative] flips immediately into fantasies of the future. Not only does this reinforce the hegemonic ideology of technological progress, but it still leaves the present essentially untouched.'[7]

Noble is probably right with respect to most technologies, but there are qualitative differences with new information technologies that he has not taken into account. For one thing, ICTs are partly malleable by definition, with the hardware – the most difficult part to adapt – constituting a common basis open to host peripherals and software, through standard connectors and communication protocols, which complete a full system that only then fulfils a number of diverse functions. The design of peripherals, and of software in particular, presents fewer difficulties, and can be accomplished relatively more quickly (even within a few months in some cases) than other advanced but not computer-based technologies.

There are already numerous examples, including the Fido telecommunication software mentioned above, developed by a single programmer in the 1980s with the explicit purpose of enabling grass-roots computer networking. By the early 1990s, multilingual computer-mediated communication was still problematic and largely neglected by commercial software developers. Yet a progressive Italian ISP, Agorà Telematica, prioritized this feature in the development of its DOS interface, and provided services for users across Europe in seven languages, including Russian in the Cyrillic alphabet.[8] The proper use of multiple languages has now been addressed by corporate investment in newer operating systems, such as the ubiquitous Windows, but Agorà's work illustrates how appropriation can increase the responsiveness of ICTs to the needs of progressive sectors, without following the trail of corporate-driven initiatives hoping for possible beneficial fallouts. The more recent burgeoning of Open Source Software – notably of the Linux operating system and its numerous applications – is another case of co-operative, partly non-commercial, technological appropriation. In early 2000, peer-to-peer Internet networking technologies allowing the location and swapping of files directly between users, without the need for a central registry, proliferated rapidly. Such software – including Napster, Freenet and Gnutella – have once more revealed the possibility of significant technological change, sometimes led by small-scale developers, which civil society sponsors and quickly appropriates. Fearing for their ability to levy copyrights, major music and software manufacturers have promptly attempted to outlaw the technology,[9] in a clear case of reaction to deviations from their own technological agenda. While this does not represent the norm, it nevertheless shows the possibility of quickly opening significant cracks in the foundation of corporate ICT development and deployment, with alternative processes and results.

Another distinction that must be made is between the spheres of application of ICTs, which, unlike some other technologies, extend to activities of both production and reproduction. In the case of automation tools, Noble notes:

No existing technologies have ever had to pass such tests of viability until (if ever) after the politically determined and culturally sanctioned decisions to invest in them had already been made, on other grounds. Thus the effort to render new alternatives realistic in economic or technical terms, already under way in several projects, is a Sisyphean task, consuming scarce resources and likely to end in frustration and cynicism. For without the requisite social power that could deem labour's alternatives viable – whatever the researchers and unions come up with will be dismissed on economic and technical grounds, but for political reasons.[10]

Since capital maintains control of most of the production process, and until that situation changes, this argument certainly remains valid for both automation and information technologies. In such cases, the most valid strategy, with both short- and long-term implications, may be digital resistance to the controlling forms and use of ICTs in production, trade, the media, and surveillance. Numerous examples of appropriation for that purpose of resistance already exist, such as browsers and websites that permit navigation with complete anonymity, thus preventing profiling and surveillance. In turn, however, as ICTs are also tools of reproduction, used by a wide range of autonomous oppositional social movements, there is also a role for alternative ICTs. Research in this area is therefore not futile, and can address a number of immediate information and communication needs among civil society organizations.

This context necessarily emphasizes that alternative

strategies must focus not only on technologies *per se*, but also – if not more importantly – on the political relations that shape their social insertion – that is, on the processes that determine the control of both the development and the content of information systems. In other words, we must refuse to 'substitute technology for politics', and 'learn not only to put technology in perspective but also to put it aside, to make way for politics. The goal must be not a human-centred technology, but a human-centred society.'[11] This implies that democratic options for ICTs and the Internet must still be bitterly struggled for. This work requires the development of a coherent information and communication strategy, based on a critical analysis and a clear political agenda. As we have seen, both the forms given to ICTs, and control over them, mostly mirror social relations at a given historical moment. Strategies of technological appropriation cannot, therefore, be taken in the abstract: a progressive use and appropriation of ICTs should be understood, and planned, and emerge, only as one of the many organic instruments available to ongoing social struggles.

Like any process of social change, technological appropriation, in this broader technological and social sense, is a struggle that can be fought without risks of co-optation only by the grass roots themselves, in defence of their own interests. This will ensure that networking activism is not a cause disembodied from its purpose, developing with its own logic and

interests, but, rather, rooted in and responsive to broader political objectives. On the one hand, this implies the rejection of
top-down approaches and externally granted 'empowerment',
often based on liberal benevolence or dubious technical assistance with more or less hidden industrial and commercial
agendas. External agents can certainly play a role, but one of
solidarity rather than leadership. Their work can contribute to
remove obstacles and make resources available, but cannot
pretend to teach and steer grass-roots sectors without the risk of
distorting, sooner or later, a project of emancipation into a
remote-controlled consolidation of subjugation co-opted by the
interests of other sectors. Intellectuals dealing with technologies, for their part, can contribute by creating space for
alternative technological appropriation through the scepticism
and questioning essential to the nurturing of democratic
debates. This permits a demystifying of ICTs and the information society fanfare, while it sheds light on the hidden but no
less real motivations and processes behind the development of
the so-called *new economy*. Intellectuals must openly question:

> the causal connections between investment, innovation, produc-
> tivity, competitiveness and social welfare. Any serious
> present-tense assessment of new technologies would readily reveal
> the fragility of assumed justifications. Contrast this with the clear-
> cut social costs entailed in the corporate-sponsored application of
> new technology, including structural unemployment, social

dislocation, job degradation, worker deskilling, and political insta-
bility. It must fall to the ideologues of progress to prove, rather than
simply assume, the benefits *before* they are allowed to proceed.[12]

On the other hand, electronic networking should be seen as a
continuation and consolidation of existing information practices. Both urban and rural poor, for example, already have
elaborate survival strategies that include organic information
systems and networks:

> What seems to be called for is an articulation between local know-
> ledge systems and the new ICTs so that the latter simply build on
> the efficiency, effectiveness, flexibility and sustainability increas-
> ingly apparent in the former. The interface must be directed by
> local groups, though, to avoid the dangers of appropriation, impo-
> sition and general ignorance.'[13]

From such a grass-roots-grounded strategy, if progressive grass-
roots sectors are able to consolidate and improve organic
information systems – responding to the needs of peasants,
small traders, prostitutes, or street children, for example – then
ICTs may start benefiting them more than they perpetuate their
alienation.

The seizing of opportunities, and genuine civil society initiatives in technology appropriation, have already been critical
in making ICTs more useful. Over the last two decades, the
tenacious dedication of social movements, systemic solidarity,

and spontaneous generosity have helped in the development of grass-roots computer networking, and they continue to provide much non-commercial online dynamism within and between civil society organizations. Many providers have conducted research, established alternative technical and information services, and facilitated user appropriation of computer networks. They have been committed to raising awareness, improving the networking of information, providing access and training facilities, and bypassing secure gateways and other information filters, while setting up electronic resources and archives, fora of alternative information sharing, and autonomous utilities for online resource location. Examples include the APC and other civil society service providers mentioned earlier. Others are communication bridges such as rebroadcasting through community radio, street theatres,[14] and public libraries.[15] There are also support centres that provide information, technical and financial services, and translate 'between technical issues and legal issues, between the dynamics of systems and the dynamics of communities, between technological visions and social visions'.[16] While these progressive civil society networking organizations suffer increasingly from marginalization, they remain pivotal if an alternative development and use of ICTs are to be possible at all. Alternative providers, being too faint in a sky of largely commercial ISPs, can barely challenge the hegemony of mainstream media, but they can still circulate critical information to those willing to listen and act upon it.

Yet this political strategy is under great pressure, and must be pursued and reinforced as an enduring effort of appropriation that meets the specific and changing needs of the grass roots, while taking advantage of their resources and strengths. Progressive activism remains essential in enfranchising ICTs, freeing them of oppressive characteristics, making them serve emancipation, and preventing the asphyxia, co-option, or ostracism of alternative options. To be of relevance to progressive grass roots and activists, ICT-based information systems must therefore clearly identify the circumstances of those sectors, and address them with appropriate content and forms. A computer networking strategy needs to begin with an information audit covering current information practices and an assessment of needs, constraints and opportunities, and an appraisal of the old and new tools by which grass-roots sectors can keep or take control of the information they have and need. This may involve considering the constraints of low-income, polyvalent, time-stretched grass-roots users and progressive civil society activists from financial, technical, organizational, political and legal angles, while identifying and taking advantage of their resources and potentials.

V

Conclusions

In the midst of the media hype and considerable analytical confusion about information and communication technologies, and the information society they supposedly beget, this book has proposed a political economy of ICTs. I look at how those technologies are actually developed, with what characteristics and implications, and in whose interest in relations of both production and reproduction.

To this end, I first examined a number of theoretical perspectives on the relationship between information technologies and society, classifying them in four broad groups. The first is *functional neutrality*, which sees technologies as neutral artefacts naturally selected by scientific and commercial processes and, as such, necessarily bearers of progress. A second approach, *instrumentalism*, acknowledges that technologies are

implemented by societies with either positive or negative implications. This choice is said to be purely social, however, leaving
technology to develop in complete independence. *Ahistorical
inherence*, as a third approach, goes one step further in seeing
technologies as inherently political by nature. This means that
they are not neutral instruments but in fact have embedded
characteristics that influence their social impact. It is from this
perspective that much of the literature on ICTs has enthusias-
tically seen these technologies as tools of liberation,
emphasizing networking processes and thus being inherently
participatory, co-operative, a threat to hierarchies, and difficult
to control centrally. It is the fourth approach, *historical inherence*, however, that completes the tools of analysis by explicitly
questioning the very process by which these embedded characteristics actually appear in the first place. This perspective
therefore defines technologies as fields of social struggle
shaped by the interests of various groups, where technologies
are intentionally developed with certain given characteristics
rather than others. Such an analysis lays the basis for examin-
ing ICTs, and the various forms of information they manipulate,
in the light of their relations to broader political economic
processes and interests.

From there, I went on to ask why ICTs are being developed
as they are, and how, as a result, they affect social relations. I
approached these questions from four different angles, each

corresponding to a different type of information that ICTs currently handle: production information (embedded in production processes and tools), circulation information (relative to marketing), media content (as both commodities and discourses), and reproduction information (carrying ideologies or allowing surveillance and repression). In relation to labour processes, ICTs are generally presented as tools that increase productivity. However, their impact on productivity is in fact questionable. I argued that the emphasis on productivity obfuscates the fact that ICTs are also tools of labour control which permit capital to subsume the workforce further in relations of production, thus increasing surplus-labour extraction and profitability, irrespective of productivity.

In the sphere of circulation, ICTs are said to reduce transaction costs and empower consumers by enabling friction-free capitalism. Yet I have shown here that the marketing patterns and monopolistic behaviour of the old economy are fully reproduced – and actually reinforced – in the new economy, shaping and making use of ICTs for consumer subjugation rather than empowerment.

Information technologies are also said to contribute to the democratization of information by broadening access to and diversifying media sources. Here, my analysis questioned this view by arguing that the Internet, in particular, is increasingly dominated by high-value-added media oligopolies that reproduce control and streamline mechanisms previously found in conventional media.

Finally, the dominant discourse claims that ICTs, and computer networking in particular, prevent censorship and monitoring of information, eroding the ability of authoritarian states, monopolistic corporations and other ideological gate-keepers to control discourses and repress dissent. In fact, however, I have argued that digital convergence of different ICTs is making surveillance ever more pervasive and efficient. As a result, both the technologies and the information content of computer networking are being censored, monitored and regulated by dominant sectors to ensure their ideological and political dominance. Under authoritarian and liberal regimes alike, power-holders not only dominate the ICT agenda but also have the means to obstruct alternative options, making it increasingly difficult to overcome narrowly defined ideological and political parameters, and use technologies for emancipation.

The question I ask in this book is not, therefore, whether information technologies are good or bad, as much of the literature asks, but how certain groups within societies actually form and appropriate ICTs. Whatever enhanced labour productivity information technologies bring, and whatever potential they offer for linking consumers, freeing alternative discourses, and empowering citizens, I argue here that the

101

current development of information and communication technologies has other motivations, which need to be explored and
understood in their broader political and economic context. In
fact, ICTs serve capitalist accumulation, its globalization, the
subjugation of labour, the manipulation of consumers, the hege-
monization of discourse, the surveillance of citizens and the
repression of dissent rather well. They therefore contribute little
to equity and democracy. The information revolution and its
ICT bandwagon are poor servants of social justice, and should
thus be exposed for what they really are.

If this process is to be fully understood, it also needs to be
situated in the wider context of the so-called information revolution by which a new post-Fordist regime of global
accumulation is being installed, and in which ICTs are highly
instrumental.[1] Through neo-liberalism and flexible accumulation, new regulations are being established to reconstitute
capitalist relations of power at the global level, beyond a re-
defined nation-state. With globalization, production is
delocalized, trade and investment are liberalized, and labour
is fragmented. Capital has also addressed its conflicts with
political opponents by moving to a new battleground, dimin-
ishing the role of the state as an arena of political
confrontation, and manoeuvring beyond the reach of those
opponents. This process permits the formation of a new breed
of virtual capitalist community which Manuel Castells situates

in a 'space of flows' (in opposition to 'spaces of places') inter-
acting in 'timeless time' (no longer sequentially binding clock
time).[2]

On the one hand, this does nothing to reduce the power of
capital, as 'the command-and-control functions of the new,
global information capitalism are, if anything, increasingly centralized and hierarchically ordered, especially in the "global
cities" . . . that form the administrative and financial command
and control centres of global capitalism'.[3] This process implies
a relocation of the tools for capitalist domination from the more
or less democratic and sovereign state to a global network of
corporate institutions, far away from societies and the 'space of
places', where most people are still grounded. On the other
hand, the sovereignty of the state is not necessarily reduced
either: 'even to study how a particular state stands vis-à-vis
the network society involves recognizing the role of the system
of states in empowering its constituent members against other
contestants for political authority'.[4] It is not the sovereignty of
the state that is reduced so much as the sovereignty of citizens
over the state, along with the ability of individual and collective
agencies to operate within structures of production and social
reproduction. Information and communication technologies
thus reinforce existing power structures in a number of ways:
from contributing to the relocation of global policy-making
beyond state politics to the consolidation of control by capital

owners, corporate merchants, media monopolies, and the state's repressive apparatus.

The single most important historical change over the last thirty years has been the globalization process, an exercise of class struggle led by a crisis of surplus-extraction and profitability. Yet, judging from the role of states and capital in the development of new information technologies (networking in particular), the role of such technologies in globalization has been much more instrumental than catalytic. It is therefore not surprising that despite significant technological change since the 1960s, my analysis finds that ICTs have brought no fundamental shift in the logic of capital accumulation – that is, its relations of production and reproduction. The forms and balance of those relations have varied, but not their nature: the roles of workers, capitalists, managers, bureaucrats, merchants, peasants, women, men, youth, ethnic groups, or castes have remained basically unchanged, while ICTs mostly serve the intensification of exploitative and oppressive relations between those social sectors.

In short, to the extent that they facilitate control, ICTs are obviously of little help in the economic and political emancipation of labour, consumers, and citizens. This is particularly true for the most deprived sectors: subsistence peasants, the urban homeless, illiterates, unskilled workers, exploited ethnic minorities and oppressed women whose information needs are rarely addressed by mainstream systems, whether electronic or not. ICTs exist to benefit not only the bourgeois and managerial classes of industrialized countries but also the large-scale merchants, bureaucrats, conservative and patriarchal ideologues, caciques, landlords and professional elites of all societies. And in fact, attempts to develop non-commercial civil society networks in many Third World countries have had mixed results, mostly serving development agencies, their employees, and their closer national counterparts, media correspondents, foreign corporate representatives, university researchers and contractors, tourist offices and others in the business sector.[5]

Yet, as indicated in the theoretical discussion on technologies, ICTs do not determine social processes. It is social processes that define how ICTs develop, and to what use they are being put. The trends analyzed above are therefore not irremediable, and other paths are still possible. Chapter IV discussed the key points of possible alternative strategies, warning of their limitations and emphasizing the need for political objectives and struggles to determine the nature of technological appropriation. Progressive organizations will continue to adopt information and communication strategies coherent with their political objectives, establishing and supporting alternative information providers, developers, and ISPs, while disseminating their own valuable information to others.

But as the technology continues to evolve rapidly, new technical, organizational, political and legal tools will be needed to bypass and confront the restrictions and agendas on hardware, software and information flows that dominant groups and state authorities are now successfully imposing.

Notes

I Introduction

1. See especially Frances Cairncross, *The Death of Distance: How the Communications Revolution Will Change Our Lives*, London, Orion Business Books, 1997; Daniel F. Burton Jr, 'The Brave New Wired World', *Foreign Policy* (Washington), no. 106, Spring 1997, pp. 23–37; Nicholas Negroponte, *Being Digital*, London, Coronet, 1995; Erick Flakoll A, 'Democracia cibernética', *Pensamiento Propio*, no. 105, August 1993, pp. 17–24; Sheldon Annis, 'Giving Voice to the Poor', *Foreign Policy* (Washington), no. 84, Fall 1991, pp. 93–106; Jessica Lipnack and Jeffrey Stamps, *The Network Book: People Connecting With People*, New York, Routledge & Kegan Paul, 1986; 'Liberty.com', *The Economist*, 30 October 1999.
2. See especially Ziauddin Sardar and Jerome R. Ravetz (eds), *Cyberfutures: Culture and Politics on the Information Superhighway*, London, Pluto Press, 1996; Theodore Roszak, 'Dumbing Us Down', *New Internationalist*, Issue 286, December

1996; George Spencer, 'Microcybernetics as the Meta-Technology of Pure Control', in Sardar and Ravetz (eds), *Cyberfutures*, pp. 61–89; Ken Hirschkop, 'Democracy and the New Technologies', *Monthly Review*, vol. 48, no. 3, July–August 1996, pp. 86–98.

3. Robert Cox, quoted in G.R.D. Underhill, 'Conceptualizing the Changing Global Order', pp. 17–44 in R. Stubbs and G.R.D. Underhill (eds.), *Political Economy and the Changing Global Order*, London, Macmillan, 1994, p. 22.

II Discourse of Machines and Machines of Discourse

1. See especially Cees Hamelink, 'New Information and Communication Technologies: Social Development and Cultural Change', Geneva, United Nations Research Institute for Social Development, Discussion Paper no. 86, 1997, p. 3.
2. See especially Jean L. Cohen and Andrew Arato, *Civil Society and Political Theory*, Cambridge, MA, MIT Press, 1994, p. 143; Neera Chandhoke, *State and Civil Society: Explorations in Political Theory*, New Delhi, Sage, 1995, pp. 148–54; Keith Tester, *Civil Society*, London, Routledge, 1992, pp. 138–43; Fernando Calderón, Alejandro Piscitelli and José Luís Reyna, 'Social Movements: Actors, Theories, Expectations', pp. 19–36 in Arturo Escobar and Sonia E. Alvarez (eds), *The Making of Social Movements in Latin America: Identity, Strategy and Democracy*, Boulder, CO, Westview Press, 1992, p. 28.
3. Ellen Meiksins Wood, 'The Uses and Abuses of Civil Society', pp. 60–84 in Ralph Miliband, Leo Panitch and John Saville (eds), *Socialist Register 1990*, London, Merlin Press, 1990, p. 74.
4. See especially Vincent Mosco, *The Political Economy of Communication: Rethinking and Renewal*, London, Sage, 1996, p. 65.

5. Vincent Mosco, 'Political Economy, Communication, and Labor', pp. 13–38 in Gerald Sussman and John A. Lent (eds), *Global Productions: Labor in the Making of the 'Information Society'*, Cresskill, NJ, Hampton Press. 1998, p. 22.

6. Robert W. McChesney, 'The Political Economy of Global Communication', pp. 1–26 in Robert W. McChesney, Ellen Meiksins Wood and John Bellamy Foster, *Capitalism and the Information Age: The Political Economy of the Global Communication Revolution*, New York, Monthly Review Press, 1998 (p. 8).

7. Richard Heeks presents a different but useful charted categorization of such analyses. In his model, one axis scales the impact of ICT from pessimism, to neutrality, to optimism; the other classifies the causes of such impact from technological to social determinist, with contingency in between (Richard Heeks, 'Information and Communication Technologies, Poverty and Development', Institute for Development Policy and Management, University of Manchester, Development Informatics Working Paper Series, Working Paper No. 5, 1999, p. 14; http://www.man.ac.uk/idpm/diwpf5.htm).

8. Andrew Feenberg, *Critical Theory of Technology*, New York, Oxford University Press, 1991, pp. 7–8.

9. Langdon Winner, *The Whale and the Reactor: A Search for Limits in an Age of High Technology*, Chicago and London, University of Chicago Press, 1986, p. 108.

10. See David F. Noble, *America by Design: Science, Technology, and the Rise of Corporate Capitalism*, New York, Alfred A. Knopf, 1977; Feenberg, *Critical Theory of Technology*; and Vandana Shiva, 'The Politics of the Green Revolution', *Third World Resurgence*, no. 33, May 1993, pp. 4–8.

11. Winner, *The Whale and the Reactor*, p. 108.

12. David F. Noble, *Progress Without People: New Technologies,*

Unemployment, and the Message of Resistance, Toronto, Between the Lines, 1995, p. 6.

13. Winner, *The Whale and the Reactor*, p. 108; Hamelink, 'New Information and Communication Technologies', pp. 18–20.

14. Sheldon Annis, 'Giving Voice to the Poor', *Foreign Policy* (Washington), no. 84, Fall 1991, pp. 93–106; Lawrence T. Greenberg and Seymour E. Goodman, 'Is Big Brother Hanging by His Bootstraps?', *Communications of the ACM*, vol. 39, no. 7, July 1996, pp. 11–15; Frances Cairncross, *The Death of Distance: How the Communications Revolution Will Change Our Lives*, London, Orion Business Books, 1997, pp. 252–3.

15. Noble, *Progress Without People*, pp. 71–2.

16. S.M. Ghazanfar, 'Third World Technological Change: Some Perspectives on Socio-economic Implications', *The Journal of Social, Political and Economic Studies*, vol. 15, no. 1, Spring 1990, pp. 91–105.

17. Feenberg, *Critical Theory of Technology*, p. 5.

18. David F. Noble, *Forces of Production: A Social History of Industrial Automation*, New York, Alfred A. Knopf, 1984, pp. 144–5; Shiva, 'The Politics of the Green Revolution'.

19. Winner, *The Whale and the Reactor*, pp. 37–8.

20. Cairncross, *The Death of Distance*, pp. 148, 257.

21. Jessica Lipnack and Jeffrey Stamps, *The Network Book: People Connecting With People*, New York, Routledge & Kegan Paul, 1986; Annis, 'Giving Voice to the Poor'; Eric Lee, *The Labour Movement and the Internet: The New Internationalism*, London, Pluto Press, 1997.

22. Winner, *The Whale and the Reactor*, pp. 95–6.

23. From Daniel Boorstin's *The Republic of Technology*, cited in ibid., p. 20.

24. Gerald Sussman, *Communication, Technology, and Politics in the Information Age*, Thousand Oaks, Sage, CA 1997, pp. 23–9.

25. Winner, *The Whale and the Reactor*, pp. 79–80.

26. Michael Dawson and John Bellamy Foster, 'Virtual Capitalism: The Political Economy of the Information Highway', *Monthly Review*, vol. 48, no. 3, July–August 1996, pp. 40–58 (p. 42).

27. Manuel Castells, *The Informational City: Information Technology, Economic Restructuring, and the Urban–Regional Process*, Oxford, Basil Blackwell, 1989, p. 8, citing Daniel Bell, *The Coming of Post-Industrial Society*, 1973, p. 29.

28. Frances Stewart, *Technology and Underdevelopment*, London, Macmillan, 1978, pp. 4–10.

29. Noble, *America by Design*, p. xxii.

30. Feenberg, *Critical Theory of Technology*, p. 14; Andrew Gillespie and Kevin Robins, 'Geographical Inequalities: The Spatial Bias of the New Communications Technologies', *Journal of Communication*, vol. 39, no. 3, Summer 1989, pp. 7–18 (8–9).

31. Gerald Sussman, *The Political Economy of Telecommunication Transfer: Transnationalizing the New Philippines Information Order*, Ph.D. dissertation, University of Hawaii, 1983, p. 208.

32. Noble, *Forces of Production*, p. 146.

33. Stewart, *Technology and Underdevelopment*, pp. 110–11.

34. Noble, *Forces of Production*, pp. 55–6; Mitka Das and Shinley Kolack, *Technology, Values and Society: Social Forces in Technological Change*, New York, Peter Lang, 1989, p. 9.

35. Noble, *America by Design*; Winner, *The Whale and the Reactor*, p. 25.

36. Stewart, *Technology and Underdevelopment*, p. 111; Noble, *Forces of Production*, p. 195.

37. Winner, *The Whale and the Reactor*, p. 55.

38. Heather Menzies, *Whose Brave New World? The Information Highway and the New Economy*, Toronto, Between the Lines, 1996, p. 27.

39. Vincent Mosco, 'Computers and Democracy', pp. 215–31 in

Jacques Berleur *et al.* (eds), *The Information Society: Evolving Landscapes*, New York, Springer-Verlag and Captus University Publishers, 1990, p. 220.

40. Bruce Girard (ed.), *A Passion for Radio*, Montreal, Black Rose Books, 1992.
41. For more historical details on the Internet, see Barry Leiner *et al.*, 'A Brief History of the Internet', *Internet Society*, 1997, http://www.isoc.org/internet/history/.
42. Cairncross, *The Death of Distance*, pp. 266–70. Contrary to the belief that e-commerce will make taxation inherently difficult, it may, on the contrary, bring the levying of taxes to unprecedented refinements. Electronic transactions are ultimately much more susceptible than cash ones to being fully monitored and controlled. In fact, it would not be surprising to see the use of cash transactions eliminated, if not criminalized altogether, over the next decades.
43. Manuel Castells, *End of Millennium*, Oxford, Basil Blackwell, 1998, pp. 168, 349.
44. James B. Cowie, 'Entering the Information Age: Implications for Developing Countries', *IEEE Technology and Society*, vol. 8, no. 4, December 1989, pp. 21–4; Jill Hills, 'The Telecommunication Rich and Poor', *Third World Quarterly*, vol. 12, no. 2, April 1990, pp. 71–90 (p. 76).
45. Vincent Mosco and Andrew Herman, 'Radical Social Theory and the Communications Revolution', pp. 58–84 in Emile G. McAnany, Jorge Schnitman and Noreene Janus (eds), *Communication and Social Structure: Critical Studies in Mass Media Research*, New York, Praeger, 1981, p. 62; CSE Microelectronic Group, *Microelectronics: Capitalist Technology and the Working Class*, London, CSE Microelectronic Group, 1980, p. 103; David Bell, 'Communication Technology – For Better or for Worse?', pp. 34–50 in Jerry L. Salvaggio (ed.),

Telecommunications: Issues and Choices for Society, New York, Longman, 1983 (p. 38).

46. Herbert I. Schiller, *Information and the Crisis Economy*, Norwood, NJ, Ablex, 1984, pp. 49–53.

47. Frédéric F. Clairmonte, 'Hors de tout contrôle, le pouvoir financier', *Manière de Voir 18 (Le Monde Diplomatique): Les frontières de l'économie globale*, May 1993, p. 21.

48. Thomas Friedman, *The Lexus and the Olive Tree*, London, HarperCollins, 1999. p. xv.

49. Sussman, *Communication, Technology, and Politics in the Information Age*, p. 38.

50. Castells, *The Informational City*, p. 26.

51. Michèle Martin, *Communication and Social Forms: A Study of the Development of the Telephone System, 1876–1920*, Ph.D. dissertation, University of Toronto, 1987, pp. 54–7; Manuel Castells, 'The Informational Economy and the New International Division of Labor', pp. 15–43 in Martin Carnoy, Manuel Castells, Stephen S. Cohen and Fernando Henrique Cardoso (eds), *The New Global Economy in the Information Age*, University Park, PA, Pennsylvania State University Press/Basingstoke, Macmillan, 1993 (p. 15); Roberto Verzola, 'Globalization: The Third Wave'. Paper presented at 'Colonialism to Globalization: Five Centuries After Vasco da Gama', New Delhi, 5 February 1998, http:/www.dkglobal.org/.

52. Sussman, *Communication, Technology, and Politics in the Information Age*, p. 173; Howard Rheingold, *The Virtual Community: Homesteading on the Electronic Frontier*, Reading, Addison-Wesley, 1993, pp. 110–44.

III Information Society or Control Society?

1. Manuel Castells, *The Informational City: Information Technology, Economic Restructuring, and the Urban–Regional Process*, Oxford, Basil Blackwell, 1989, p. 10.
2. Borrowing the concept from Alain Touraine, Castells defines modes of development as 'the technological arrangements through which labor acts upon matter to generate the product, ultimately determining the level of surplus' (*The Informational City*, p. 10).
3. Ibid., p. 13.
4. Ibid.
5. Fernando Henrique Cardoso, 'North–South Relations in the Present Context: A New Dependency', pp. 149–59 in Martin Carnoy, Manuel Castells, Stephen S. Cohen and Fernando Henrique Cardoso (eds), *The New Global Economy in the Information Age*, University Park, PA, Pennsylvania State University Press/Basingstoke, Macmillan, 1993 (p. 157).
6. Manuel Castells, *End of Millennium*, Oxford, Basil Blackwell, 1998, pp. 35–6.
7. See especially Castells, *The Informational City*, pp. 22–3; Robert Brenner, 'The Economics of Global Turbulence', *New Left Review*, 229 May–June 1998, pp. 1–264. For a critique of the concept, see especially Ellen Meiksins Wood, 'Modernity, Postmodernity, or Capitalism?', pp. 27–49 in Robert W. McChesney, Ellen Meiksins Wood and John Bellamy Foster, *Capitalism and the Information Age: The Political Economy of the Global Communication Revolution*, New York, Monthly Review Press, 1998.
8. Castells, *The Informational City*, p. 30.
9. See Eric S. Raymond, 'Homesteading the Noosphere', April 1998, http://www.tuxedo.org/~esr/writings/homesteading.

10. Vinod Valloppillil, 'Open Source Software: A (New?) Development Methodology', Leaked Internal Microsoft document, 11 August 1998.

11. From H.G. Wells (1938), quoted in Kevin Robins and Frank Webster, 'Cybernetic Capitalism: Information, Technology, Everyday Life', pp. 44–75 in Vincent Mosco and Janet Wasko (eds), *The Political Economy of Information*, Madison, University of Wisconsin Press, 1988 (p. 68).

12. Cees Hamelink, 'New Information and Communication Technologies: Social Development and Cultural Change', Geneva, United Nations Research Institute for Social Development, Discussion Paper no. 86, 1997, p. 26.

13. Robert Gordon, 'Not Much of a New Economy', *Financial Times*, 26 July 2000.

14. *The Economist*, 'Readjusting the Lens', 20 November 1999.

15. Manuel Castells, 'The Informational Economy and the New International Division of Labor', pp. 15–43 in Martin Carnoy, Manuel Castells, Stephen S. Cohen and Fernando Henrique Cardoso (eds), *The New Global Economy in the Information Age*, University Park, PA, Pennsylvania State University Press/Basingstoke, Macmillan, 1993 (p. 18).

16. David F. Noble, *Progress Without People: New Technologies, Unemployment, and the Message of Resistance*, Toronto, Between the Lines, 1995, pp. 91–4.

17. Ibid., pp. 101–7.

18. George Spencer, 'Microcybernetics as the Meta-Technology of Pure Control', pp. 61–89 in Ziauddin Sardar and Jerome R. Ravetz (eds), *Cyberfutures: Culture and Politics on the Information Superhighway*, London, Pluto Press, 1996 (p. 62).

19. In turn, *cyberspace*, now referring broadly to computer networking and virtual reality, was a rather unfortunate denomination that William Gibson himself, author of *Neuromancer* and father of

the term, admitted to be a 'neologic spasm: the primal act of pop poetics. Preceded any concept whatever. Slick and hollow - awaiting received meaning.' (Quoted in Julian Stallabrass, 'Empowering Technology: The Exploration of Cyberspace', *New Left Review*, 211, May–June 1995, p. 5.)

20. Spencer, 'Microcybernetics as the Meta-Technology of Pure Control', pp. 61–2.

21. Andrew Clement, 'Office Automation and the Technical Control of Information Workers', pp. 217–43 in Vincent Mosco and Janet Wasko (eds), *The Political Economy of Information*, Madison, University of Wisconsin Press, 1988 (p. 227).

22. David Noble, *America by Design: Science, Technology, and the Rise of Corporate Capitalism*, New York, Alfred A. Knopf, 1977.

23. Heather Menzies, *Whose Brave New World? The Information Highway and the New Economy*, Toronto, Between the Lines, 1996, p. 35.

24. Langdon Winner, *The Whale and the Reactor: A Search for Limits in an Age of High Technology*, Chicago and London, University of Chicago Press, 1986, pp. 47–8.

25. Clement, 'Office Automation and the Technical Control of Information Workers', pp. 224–33.

26. Robins and Webster, 'Cybernetic Capitalism', p. 56; Castells, *The Informational City*, pp. 29–32; Michael Gurstein, 'Information and Communications Technology and Local Economic Development: Towards a New Local Economy', in Gertrude Ann MacIntyre (ed.), *Perspectives on Communities*, Sydney, Nova Scotia, UCCB Press, 1998; Philip E. Agre, 'Surveillance and Capture: Two Models of Privacy', *The Information Society*, vol. 10, no. 2, April–June 1994, pp. 101–27.

27. Quoted from John S. Baker, 'The Luddite Tradition in the Techno Challenge', typescript, 1979, in Noble, *Progress Without People*, p. 50.

28. Menzies, *Whose Brave New World?*, p. 13.

29. Noble, *Progress Without People*, p. 80.

30. See especially ACLU (American Civil Liberties Union), 'Wayne State University Prohibits Net Use for Non-University Related Work', 5 December 1997, http://www.aclu.org/.

31. Agre, 'Surveillance and Capture'.

32. Clement, 'Office Automation and the Technical Control of Information Workers', p. 243.

33. Frances Cairncross, *The Death of Distance: How the Communications Revolution Will Change Our Lives*, London, Orion Business Books, 1997, p. 194; see also ibid., p. 274; Clement, 'Office Automation and the Technical Control of Information Workers', p. 229.

34. *The Economist*, 'Electronic Surveillance: Being Watched', 26 August 2000, p. 26.

35. Denis Duclos, 'Little Castle of the Soul', *Le Monde Diplomatique* (English edition), August 1999.

36. Clement, 'Office Automation and the Technical Control of Information Workers', p. 242.

37. Duclos, 'Little Castle of the Soul'.

38. Clement, 'Office Automation and the Technical Control of Information Workers', p. 228.

39. Mark Lebovich, 'At Amazon.com, It's a Jungle: The New Economy Needs Speed', *International Herald Tribune*, 23 November 1999, p. 2.

40. Agre, 'Surveillance and Capture'.

41. Howard Rheingold, *The Virtual Community: Finding Connection in a Computerized World*, London, Secker & Warburg, 1994, p. 88; Gerald Sussman, *Communication, Technology, and Politics in the Information Age*, Thousand Oaks, CA, Sage, 1997, p. 174.

42. Barry Leiner *et al.*, 'A Brief History of the Internet', Internet Society 1997.

43. *The Economist*, 'The Consensus Machine', 10 June 2000.

44. For updates on the ICANN confrontation relative to the creation of new top-level domain names, see Simon Craig, 'Overview of the DNS Controversy', http://www.flywheel.com/ircw/overview.html (26 March 2000).

45. *The Economist*, 'The Internet: Can You?',10 March 2000.

46. Sylvie Kauffmann,'Le cybercitoyen modèle est mâle, blanc, jeune et américain', *Le Monde (Supplément Multimédia)*, 30 September 1996, http://www.lemonde.fr/.

47. *The Economist*, 'The Internet: Can You?'.

48. *The Economist*, 'Electronic Commerce: Amazon's Delta', 20 November 1999, p. 97.

49. *The Economist*, 'Dotty about dot.commerce?', 26 February 2000, p. 19.

50. Ibid.

51. *Financial Times*, 1 December 1999, p. v; *The Economist*, 'Shopping Around the Web', 26 February 2000.

52. *The Economist*, 'Shopping Around the Web'.

53. See especially James Mackintosh, 'Customers to Benefit from Internet's Explosive Impact', *Financial Times*, 1 December 1999, p. IV.

54. *The Economist*, 'Liberty.com', 30 October 1999.

55. *The Economist*, 'Frictions in Cyberspace: Retailing on the Internet, it is said, is almost Perfectly Competitive. Really?', 20 November 1999, p. 112.

56. Peter de Jonge, 'Whiteknuckleride@amazon.com', *Daily Telegraph Magazine*, 22 August 1999, p. 45.

57. Tony Jackson, 'Safeguard Your Skills from the Cherry-pickers', *Connectis*, Issue 1, 1999.

58. *The Economist*, 'Frictions in Cyberspace, p. 112.

59. Quoted from Bob Pittman, formerly of MTC and now with AOL, in De Jonge, 'Whiteknuckleride@amazon.com', p. 45.

60. Ibid., p. 41.
61. *The Economist*, 'Frictions in Cyberspace', p. 112.
62. See especially Michael Dawson and John Bellamy Foster, 'Virtual Capitalism: Monopoly Capital, Marketing, and the Information Highway', pp. 51–67 in Robert W. McChesney, Ellen Meiksins Wood and John Bellamy Foster, *Capitalism and the Information Age: The Political Economy of the Global Communication Revolution*, New York, Monthly Review Press, 1998.
63. *The Economist*, 'Frictions in Cyberspace, p. 112.
64. Agre, 'Surveillance and Capture, pp. 101–27.
65. Terry Curtis, 'The Information Society: A Computer-Generated Caste System?' pp. 95–107 in Vincent Mosco and Janet Wasko, *The Political Economy of Information*, Madison, University of Wisconsin Press, 1988 (p. 96).
66. Ibid.
67. Caroline Daniel *et al.*, 'Books, Music and Holidays at the Click of a Mouse', *Connectis*, Issue 1, 1999, p. 50.
68. Greg Sandoval, 'Failed Dot-coms May Be Selling Your Private Information', *CNET News.com*, 29 June 2000.
69. Nick Wingfield and Glenn R. Simpson, 'AOL's Cautious Privacy Stance', *The Wall Street Journal Europe*, 16 March 2000, p. 25.
70. Ibid.
71. Curtis, 'The Information Society', p.103.
72. Ibid., p.104.
73. *The Economist*, 'Seller Beware', 4 March 2000, p. 67.
74. Patrick de Jacquelot, 'Ups and Downs of Internet Banking', *Connectis*, Issue 1, 1999, pp. 30–31.
75. Rachel Konrad, 'Net Consolidation as a Natural, Accelerated Business Cycle', *CNET News.com*, 23 June 2000.
76. *The Economist*, 'Dotty about dot.commerce?', p. 19.
77. *The Economist*, 'The Fright After Christmas', 5 February 2000.

78. Tim Jackson, 'Strong Brands Stand Tall in On-line Shake-out', *Financial Times*, 21 March 2000, p. 13; and De Jonge, 'Whiteknuckleride@amazon.com', p. 41.

79. *The Economist*, 'Dotty about dot.commerce?', p. 19.

80. Daniel *et al.*, 'Books, Music and Holidays at the Click of a Mouse', p. 50.

81. *The Economist*, 'Shopping Around the Web'.

82. Ibid.; Daniel *et al.*, 'Books, Music and Holidays at the Click of a Mouse', p. 51.

83. James Harding, 'Top of the Ratings', *Financial Times*, 16 December 1999, p. 24.

84. *The Economist*, 'Liberty.com'.

85. Thorgeir Einarsson, 'The less time people spend in front of their screens the better', *Zum Thema*, no. 37, 4 February 2000.

86. Marcus Taylor, 'Servicing the Wireless Internet Market', *Zum Thema*, no. 38, 3 March 2000, WWW-neu: Wireless Wired World.

87. Enguérand Renault, 'Fidéliser le client est désormais plus important que détenir la dernière technologie', and 'La bataille pour la troisième génération de téléphone mobile commence', *Le Monde*, 29 February 2000, p. 23.

88. Rheingold, *The Virtual Community*.

89. Ibid., p. 14; Lawrence T. Greenberg and Seymour E. Goodman, 'Is Big Brother Hanging by His Bootstraps?', *Communications of the ACM*, vol. 39, no. 7, July 1996, pp. 11–15; Eric Lee, *The Labour Movement and the Internet: The New Internationalism*, London, Pluto Press, 1997; *The Economist*, 'Citizens' Groups: The Nongovernmental Order', 11 December 1999.

90. Winner, *The Whale and the Reactor*, p. 112.

91. Madelaine Drohan, 'How the Net Killed the Mai: Grassroots Groups Used Their Own Globalization to Derail Deal', *The Globe and Mail* (Toronto), 29 April 1998.

92. See especially Simon Bromley, 'The Space of Flows and Timeless Time', *Radical Philosophy*, no. 97, September/October 1999, p. 16.

93. See Jessica Lipnack and Jeffrey Stamps, *The Network Book: People Connecting With People*, New York, Routledge & Kegan Paul, 1986; Lee, *The Labour Movement and the Internet*.

94. Robins and Webster, 'Cybernetic Capitalism', p. 69.

95. Ken Hirschkop, 'Democracy and the New Technologies', *Monthly Review*, vol. 48, no. 3, July–August 1996, pp. 86–98, (pp. 96–7); see also Peter Golding, 'World Wide Wedge: Division and Contradiction in the Global Information Infrastructure', *Monthly Review*, vol. 48, no. 3, July–August 1996, Stallabrass, 'Empowering Technology', pp. 17–18.

96. Winner, *The Whale and the Reactor*, pp. 108–9.

97. Luc Lamprière, 'Microsoft s'attaque au téléspectateur américain', *Libération*, 14 January 1998; Rheingold, *The Virtual Community*, pp. 274–5; Sussman, *Communication, Technology, and Politics in the Information Age*, pp. 141–6; Harding, 'Top of the Ratings', p. 24.

98. Herbert I. Schiller, 'La communication, une affaire d'État pour Washington', *Manière de Voir, Le Monde Diplomatique*, no. 46, July–August 1999, pp. 65–8 (p. 68).

99. Sussman, *Communication, Technology, and Politics in the Information Age*, p. 182.

100. Cairncross, *The Death of Distance*, p. 141.

101. Theodore Roszak, 'Dumbing Us Down', *New Internationalist*, Issue 286, December 1996.

102. NVision Press Release, 5 October 1999, www.nvision.co.uk/page pr 5.html.

103. See also Lee, *The Labour Movement and the Internet*, p. 171.

104. Hervé Morin, 'Le diamètre de la Toile est revu à la hausse', *Le Monde*, 2 June 2000, p. 21; T. Matthew Ciolek, 'Networked

information flows in East Asia: a pilot study on research uses of the Altavista search engine', Canberra, ANU, 10 June 2000.

105. Michael R. Ogden, 'Politics in a Parallel Universe: Is there a Future for Cyberdemocracy?', *Futures* (London), vol. 26, no. 7, September 1994, pp. 713–29 (p. 724).

106. Edward S. Herman, 'The Propaganda Model Revisited', *Monthly Review*, vol. 48, no. 3, July–August 1996, pp. 115–28 (p. 118).

107. David Kline, 'The Myth of Disintermediation', *Market Forces*, 1996, http://www.hotwired.com/.

108. *Far Eastern Economic Review*, 'Internet TV: Ready for Action', 1 June 2000.

109. Reg Whitaker, 'The Tower of Infobabel: Cyberspace as Alternative Universe', pp. 173–88 in Leo Panitch (ed.), *Socialist Register 1996: Are There Alternatives?*, London, Merlin Press, 1996 (p. 186).

110. Peter G. Neumann, 'Risks on the Information Superhighway', *Communications of the ACM*, vol. 37, no. 6, June 1994, p. 114; Mark S. Bonchek, 'Grassroots in Cyberspace: Using Computer Networks to Facilitate Political Participation', The Political Participation Project, MIT Artificial Intelligence Laboratory, Working Paper 95–2.2: Presented at the 53rd Annual Meeting of the Midwest Political Science Association in Chicago, IL, 6 April 1995.

111. *The Economist*, 'Survey: Telecommunication', 17 October 1987, p. 32.

112. Quoted in Dawson and Foster, 'Virtual Capitalism', p. 43.

113. Paul Sagawa, 'The Balkanization of the Internet', *The McKinsey Quarterly*, no. 1, 1997, pp. 127–37 (p. 134).

114. Ibid., p. 128; see also Cairncross, *The Death of Distance*, pp. 37–8, 115–16.

115. *The Economist*, 'Reuters Setting Up Shop', 12 February 2000.

116. Nick Wingfield and Glenn R. Simpson, 'AOL's Cautious Privacy

Stance', *The Wall Street Journal Europe*, 16 March 2000, p. 25; *The Economist*, 22 January 2000, p. 70.

117. Philip Manchester, 'Network Devices Challenge PC', *Financial Times*, 1 December 1999, p. IT-V.

118. Sagawa, 'The Balkanization of the Internet', p. 134; see also Leiner *et al.*, 'A Brief History of the Internet'.

119. Rheingold, *The Virtual Community*, p. 14; Charles Swett, *Strategic Assessment: The Internet*, Washington, 17 July 1995, Office of the Assistant Secretary of Defense for Special Operations and Low-Intensity Conflict (Policy Planning), Pentagon, http://www.fas.org/.

120. Cairncross, *The Death of Distance*, p. 25.

121. *The Economist*, 'Liberty.com'.

122. Nicholas Negroponte, *Being Digital*, London, Coronet, 1995, p. 158; Cairncross, *The Death of Distance*, p. 148.

123. Negroponte, *Being Digital*, pp. 57–8.

124. Lee, *The Labour Movement and the Internet*, p. 39.

125. Cairncross, *The Death of Distance*, pp. 259–65; Stephen Coleman, John Taylor and Wim van de Donk, *Parliament in the Age of the Internet*, Oxford, Oxford University Press, 1999.

126. Sussman, *Communication, Technology, and Politics in the Information Age*, p. 283.

127. Duclos, 'Little Castle of the Soul'.

128. Bonchek, 'Grassroots in Cyberspace', Howard H. Frederick, *Global Communication and International Relations*, Belmont, CA, Wadsworth, 1993, p. 236; Lee, *The Labour Movement and the Internet*, pp. 163–4.

129. Howard H. Frederick, 'Breaking the Global Information Blockade Using the Technologies of Peace and War', Conference on Computers for Social Change: Tools for Progressive Action, Hunter College, New York, 26 June 1991; Rafal Rohozinski, 'Mapping Russian Cyberspace: Perspective

on Democracy and the Net'. Paper presented at the UNRISD Conference on Information Technologies and Social Development, Geneva, 22–24 June 1998.

130. Harry Cleaver, 'The Chiapas Uprising', *Studies in Political Economy*, no. 44, Summer 1994, pp. 141–57.

131. Winner, *The Whale and the Reactor*, p. 115; Sussman, *Communication, Technology, and Politics in the Information Age*, pp. 194, 212; Michael H. Warren, 'Implementation of the Communications Assistance for Law Enforcement Act (CALEA)', Washington 23 October 1997, Statement Before the Subcommittee on Crime, Committee on the Judiciary, United States House of Representatives, http://www.fbi.gov/.

132. Wayne Arnold, 'Asia's Internet Censorship Will Be Easy to Circumvent', *The Wall Street Journal Interactive Edition* (Asia edition), 11 September 1996.

133. Peter H. Lewis, 'On-line Service Cracks Down on Junk E-mail', *International Herald Tribune*, 6 September 1996, p. 14.

134. EPIC (Electronic Privacy Information Center), *Faulty Filters: How Content Filters Block Access to Kid-Friendly Information on the Internet*, Washington, DC, December 1997.

135. Anne Beeson and Chris Hansen, *Fahrenheit 451.2: Is Cyberspace Burning? How Rating and Blocking Proposals May Torch Free Speech on the Internet*, Wye Mills, ACLU (American Civil Liberties Union), MD, 1997. http://www.aclu.org/.

136. ACLU (American Civil Liberties Union) 'New ACLU Report Condemns Mandatory Blocking Software in Public Libraries', 17 June 1998, http://www.aclu.org/.

137. Francis Deron, 'Pékin met la multimédiatisation sous haute surveillance', *Le Monde*, *Supplément Multimédia*, 30 September 1996; François Fortier, *Civil Society Computer Networks: The Perilous Road of Cyber-Politics*, Ph.D. dissertation, Toronto, York University, 1997; *Reporter Sans Frontière*,

Communiqué de presse, 'Les vingt ennemis d'Internet', 9 August 1999.

138. Arnold, 'Asia's Internet Censorship Will Be Easy to Circumvent'.

139. Christopher Walker, 'Orthodox Jews Go Surfing on the Kosher Internet', *The Times* (London), 21 October 1996, p. 12.

140. EPIC, *Faulty Filters*.

141. ACLU (American Civil Liberties Union) 'Internet Free Expression Alliance Counters Censorware Summit', 5 December 1997.

142. GLAAD (Gay and Lesbian Alliance Against Defamation), *Access Denied: An Impact of Internet Filtering Software on the Gay and Lesbian Community*, 1997, http://www.glaad.org/glaad/ access_denied/.

143. Beeson and Hansen, *Fahrenheit 451.2*.

144. Rheingold, *The Virtual Community*, p. 5.

145. Quoted from Bill Truesdell, director of international operations at Compuserve, in Rob Lemos, 'Will China Squash Hong Kong's Net Freedoms?', *ZDNet*, 30 June 1997.

146. *The Economist* has an unequivocal opinion on the subject, and wrote: [Contrary to much nerdish opinion] this domain [cyberspace] can, will and should be regulated, just like other media from magazines to television' (6 January 1996, p. 18). Most importantly, the article argues that due to the legal and technical complexity of restricting and policing what is put on the Internet, liability should rest on the end-user: 'regulation ought to be at the point of delivery, not origin – to control, if need be, what people take off the Internet, not what they put on it' (ibid.). Surfers beware! Don't click the wrong icon.

147. Dinah PoKempner, 'Encryption in the Service of Human Rights', Briefing Paper, Human Rights Watch, 1 August 1997, http://www.aaas.org/SPP/DSPP/CSTC/briefings/crypto/dinah.htm.

148. Lionel Thoumyre, *Abuses in the Cyberspace: The Regulation of Illicit Messages Diffused on the Internet*, Master of Arts, ESST, Université Louis Pasteur, Strasbourg, Faculté Notre Dame de la Paix, CRID, Namur, 1996, pp. 57–63; Valérie Sédallian, 'Controlling illegal content over the Internet: the French situation'. Paper presented at 'Censoring the Internet: a lawyer's deceit', Media Law Committee, 26th International Bar Association Conference, Berlin, 23 October 1996; Yaman Akdeniz, 'Pornography on the Internet', *L'Internet Juridique*, 1996.

149. Lee, *The Labour Movement and the Internet*, p. 172.

150. Valérie Sédallian, 'Cryptographie: les enjeux et l'état de la législation française', *L'Internet Juridique*, 1997; for US-related documentation, see EPIC (Electronic Privacy Information Center), 'Former Secrets: Documents Released Under the FOIA', 1998. See also Declan McCullagh, 'U.S. Wants to Trace Net Users', *Wired*, 4 March 2000, http://www.wired.com/news/print/0,1294,34720,00.html.

151. *The Economist*, 'The Consensus Machine'.

152. Wayne Madson, 'Cryptography and Liberty: An International Survey of Encryption Policy', GILC (Global Internet Liberty Campaign), 1997.

153. Sédallian, 'Cryptographie: les enjeux et l'état de la législation française'.

154. OECD (Organization for Economic Co-operation and Development), 'OECD Adopts Guidelines For Cryptography Policy', News Release, 27 March 1997.

155. *The Economist*, 'Electronic Surveillance: Being Watched', p. 27.

156. Cairncross, *The Death of Distance*, p. 257.

157. See especially Robins and Webster, 'Cybernetic Capitalism', p. 61.

IV Alternative Strategies

1. See Douglas Schuler, *New Community Networks: Wired for Change*, Reading, Addison-Wesley, 1996, p. 274.

2. See especially Hilda Munyua, 'Application of Information Communication Technologies in the Agricultural Sector in Africa: A Gender Perspective with Special Reference to Women'. Paper presented at the United Nations Economic Commission for Africa (UNECA) International Conference on African Women and Economic Development, 1998, para. 62.

3. From Brian Murphy, quoted in Cristina Inoue, 'Organizações Não-governamentais e Redes de Comunicação', MA Thesis in International Relations, Universidade de Brasília, 1995, p. 90.

4. Langdon Winner, *The Whale and the Reactor: A Search for Limits in an Age of High Technology*, Chicago and London, University of Chicago Press, 1986, p. 80; emphasis added.

5. David Noble, *Progress Without People: New Technologies, Unemployment, and the Message of Resistance*, Toronto, Between the Lines, 1995, pp. 34–5.

6. Ibid., p. 36.

7. Ibid.

8. François Fortier, *Civil Society Computer Networks: The Perilous Road of Cyber-Politics*, Ph.D. dissertation, Toronto, York University, 1997.

9. Louise Kehoe, 'Inside Track: AppleSoup's recipe for revenue: A breakaway from Napster's music website aims to make file-swapping a profitable enterprise', *Financial Times*, 20 July 2000.

10. Noble, *Progress Without People*, p. 38.

11. Ibid., p. 66.

12. Ibid., pp. 62–3.

13. Cathy-Mae Karelse, 'Reconceptualising Education for the

Production, Use and Management of ICTs', IDRC contribution to UNECA International Conference on African Women and Economic Development, 1998, para. 26.

14. Sophia Huyer, 'Supporting Women's Use of Information Technologies for Sustainable Development', Ottawa. Submitted to the Gender and Sustainable Development Unit, IDRC, 1997. See also Munyua, 'Application of Information Communication Technologies in the Agricultural Sector in Africa', para. 29; Karelse, 'Reconceptualising Education for the Production, Use and Management of ICTs'; Don Richardson, 'The Internet and Rural Development: Recommendations for Strategy and Activity', *SD Dimensions* (FAO), August 1996.

15. UNESCO, *Information and Communication Technologies in Development: A UNESCO Perspective*, Paris UNESCO Secretariat, 1996, paras 14–15.

16. Philip E. Agre, 'The Next Internet Hero', *Technology Review*, November–December 1997.

V Conclusions

1. See especially Andrew Clement, 'Office Automation and the Technical Control of Information Workers', pp. 217–43 in Vincent Mosco and Janet Wasko (eds), *The Political Economy of Information*, Madison, University of Wisconsin Press, 1988 (p. 219), on the contribution of ICTs to the resolution of the Fordist crisis.

2. Manuel Castells, *The Informational City: Information Technology, Economic Restructuring and the Urban–Regional Process*, Oxford, Basil Blackwell, 1989, p. 348.

3. Simon Bromley, 'The Space of Flows and Timeless Time', *Radical Philosophy*, no. 97, September/October 1999, p. 11.

4. Ibid., p. 16.
5. See especially Robin van Koert, 'Bustling and Sprawling Cities: A Natural Environment for ICTs'. Working paper available at http://dkglobal.org/crit-ict, 1998; Don Richardson, 'The Internet and Rural Development: Recommendations for Strategy and Activity', *SD Dimensions* (FAO), August 1996; François Fortier, 'Living with Cyberspace: Vietnam's Latest Dilemma', pp. 237–45 in Dan Duffy (ed.), *North Viet Nam Now: Fiction and Essays from Ha Noi* (Viet Nam Forum 15), New Haven, CT, Yale University Press, 1996.

Bibliography

ACLU (American Civil Liberties Union), 'Internet Free Expression Alliance Counters Censorware Summit', 5 December 1997.

ACLU (American Civil Liberties Union), 'Wayne State University Prohibits Net Use for Non-University Related Work', 5 December 1997.

ACLU (American Civil Liberties Union), 'New ACLU Report Condemns Mandatory Blocking Software in Public Libraries', 17 June 1998.

Afonso, Carlos A., 'Au service de la société civile: réseaux électroniques et action politique', *Le Monde Diplomatique*, vol. 41 no. 484, July 1994, pp. 16–17.

Agre, Philip E., 'Surveillance and Capture: Two Models of Privacy', *The Information Society*, vol. 10, no. 2, April–June 1994, pp. 101–27.

Agre, Philip E., 'The Next Internet Hero', *Technology Review*, November–December 1997.

Akdeniz, Yaman, 'Pornography on the Internet', *L'Internet Juridique*, 1996.

Annis, Sheldon, 'Giving Voice to the Poor', *Foreign Policy* (Washington), no. 84, Fall 1991, pp. 93–106.

Arnold, Wayne, 'Asia's Internet Censorship Will Be Easy to Circumvent', *The Wall Street Journal Interactive Edition* (Asia edition), 11 September 1996.

Baran, Nicholas, 'Privatization of Telecommunication', *Monthly Review*, vol. 48, no. 3, July–August 1996, pp. 59–69.

Beeson, Anne, and Chris Hansen, *Fahrenheit 451.2: Is Cyberspace Burning? How Rating and Blocking Proposals May Torch Free Speech on the Internet*, Wye Mills, MD, ACLU, 1997.

Bell, David, 'Communication Technology – For Better or for Worse?', pp. 34–50 in Jerry L. Salvaggio (ed.), *Telecommunications: Issues and Choices for Society*, New York, Longman, 1983.

Berleur, Jacques, *et al.* (eds), *The Information Society: Evolving Landscapes*, New York, Springer-Verlag and Captus University Publishers, 1990.

Bonchek, Mark S., 'Grassroots in Cyberspace: Using Computer Networks to Facilitate Political Participation', The Political Participation Project, MIT Artificial Intelligence Laboratory, Working Paper 95–2.2. Presented at the 53rd Annual Meeting of the Midwest Political Science Association in Chicago, IL, 6 April 1995.

Brenner, Robert, 'The Economics of Global Turbulence', *New Left Review*, 229, May–June 1998, pp. 1–264.

Breton, Philippe, 'Informatique et utopie: quand s'usent les idéaux', *Le Monde Diplomatique*, vol. 40, no. 470, May 1993, p. 32.

Bromley, Simon, 'The Space of Flows and Timeless Time', *Radical Philosophy*, no. 97, September/October 1999.

Burton, Daniel F. Jr, 'The Brave New Wired World', *Foreign Policy* (Washington), no. 106, Spring 1997, pp. 23–37.

Cairncross, Frances, *The Death of Distance: How the Communications Revolution Will Change Our Lives*, London, Orion Business Books, 1997.

Calderón, Fernando, Alejandro Piscitelli and José Luís Reyna, 'Social Movements: Actors, Theories, Expectations', pp. 19–36 in Arturo Escobar and Sonia E. Alvarez (eds), *The Making of Social Movements in Latin America: Identity, Strategy and Democracy*, Boulder, CO, Westview Press, 1992.

Cardoso, Fernando Henrique, 'North-South Relations in the Present Context: A New Dependency', pp. 149–59 in Martin Carnoy, Manuel Castells, Stephen S. Cohen and Fernando Henrique Cardoso (eds), *The New Global Economy in the Information Age*, University Park, PA, Pennsylvania State University Press/Basingstoke, Macmillan, 1993.

Carnoy, Martin, Manuel Castells, Stephen S. Cohen and Fernando Henrique Cardoso (eds), *The New Global Economy in the Information Age*, University Park, PA, Pennsylvania State University Press/Basingstoke, Macmillan, 1993.

Castells, Manuel, *The Informational City: Information Technology, Economic Restructuring, and the Urban–Regional Process*, Oxford, Basil Blackwell, 1989.

Castells, Manuel, 'The Informational Economy and the New International Division of Labor', pp. 15-43 in Martin Carnoy, Manuel Castells, Stephen S. Cohen and Fernando Henrique Cardoso (eds), *The New Global Economy in the Information Age*, University Park, PA, Pennsylvania State University Press/Basingstoke, Macmillan, 1993.

Castells, Manuel, *End of Millennium*, Oxford, Basil Blackwell, 1998.

Chandhoke, Neera, *State and Civil Society: Explorations in Political Theory*, New Delhi, Sage, 1995.

Chomsky, Noam, *Media Control: The Spectacular Achievements of Propaganda*, Open Magazine, Pamphlet Series, Westfield, NJ, 1991.

Ciolek, T. Matthew, 'Networked information flows in East Asia: a pilot study on research uses of the Altavista search engine', Canberra, ANU, 10 June 2000.

Clairmonte, Frédéric F., 'Hors de tout contrôle, le pouvoir financier', *Manière de Voir 18 (Le Monde Diplomatique): Les frontières de l'économie globale*, May 1993, pp. 20–21.

Cleaver, Harry, 'The Chiapas Uprising', *Studies in Political Economy*, no. 44, Summer 1994, pp. 141–57.

Clement, Andrew, 'Office Automation and the Technical Control of Information Workers', pp. 217–43 in Vincent Mosco and Janet Wasko (eds), *The Political Economy of Information*, Madison, University of Wisconsin Press, 1988.

Cohen, Jean L., and Andrew Arato, *Civil Society and Political Theory*, Cambridge, MA, MIT Press, 1994.

Cohen, Stephen S., 'Geo-Economics: Lessons from America's Mistakes', pp. 97–147 in Martin Carnoy, Manuel Castells, Stephen S. Cohen and Fernando Henrique Cardoso, *The New Global Economy in the Information Age*, University Park, PA, Pennsylvania State University Press/Basingstoke, Macmillan, 1993.

Coleman, Stephen, John Taylor and Wim van de Donk, *Parliament in the Age of the Internet*, Oxford, Oxford University Press, 1999.

Cowie, James B., 'Entering the Information Age: Implications for Developing Countries', *IEEE Technology and Society*, vol. 8, no. 4, December 1989, pp. 21–4.

Craig, Simon, 'Overview of the DNS Controversy', http://www.fly-wheel.com/ircw/overview.html (26 March 2000).

CSE Microelectronic Group, *Microelectronics: Capitalist Technology and the Working Class*, London, CSE Microelectronic Group, 1980.

Curtis, Terry, 'The Information Society: A Computer-Generated Caste System?,' pp. 95–107 in Vincent Mosco and Janet Wasko (eds), *The Political Economy of Information*, Madison, University of Wisconsin Press, 1988.

Daniel, Caroline, *et al.*, 'Books, Music and Holidays at the Click of a Mouse', *Connectis*, Issue 1, 1999.

Das, Mitka and Shinley Kolack, *Technology, Values and Society: Social Forces in Technological Change*, New York, Peter Lang, 1989.

Dawson, Michael and John Bellamy Foster, 'Virtual Capitalism: The Political Economy of the Information Highway', *Monthly Review*, vol. 48, no. 3, July–August 1996, pp. 40–58.

Dawson, Michael, and John Bellamy Foster, 'Virtual Capitalism: Monopoly Capital, Marketing, and the Information Highway', pp. 51–67 in Robert W. McChesney, Ellen Meiksins Wood and John Bellamy Foster, *Capitalism and the Information Age: The Political Economy of the Global Communication Revolution*, New York, Monthly Review Press, 1998.

de Jacquelot, Patrick, 'Ups and Downs of Internet Banking', *Connectis*, Issue 1, 1999, pp. 30–31.

de Jonge, Peter, 'Whiteknuckleride@amazon.com', *Daily Telegraph Magazine*, 22 August 1999.

Deron, Francis, 'Pékin met la multimédiatisation sous haute surveillance', *Le Monde, Supplément Multimédia*, 30 September 1996.

Downing, John D.H., 'Computers for Political Change: PeaceNet and Public Data Access', *Journal of Communication*, vol. 39, no. 3, Summer 1989, pp. 154–62.

Drohan, Madelaine, 'How the Net Killed the Mai: Grassroots Groups Used Their Own Globalization to Derail Deal', *The Globe and Mail* (Toronto), 29 April 1998.

Duclos, Denis, 'Little Castle of the Soul', *Le Monde Diplomatique* (English edition), August 1999.

Einarsson, Thorgeir, 'The less time people spend in front of their screens the better', *Zum Thema*, no. 37, 4 February 2000.

EPIC (Electronic Privacy Information Center), 'Georgia Tech Releases New Net Survey', EPIC Alert, vol. 4, no. 9, 18 June 1997.

EPIC (Electronic Privacy Information Center), *Faulty Filters: How Content Filters Block Access to Kid-Friendly Information on the Internet*, Washington, DC, December 1997.

EPIC (Electronic Privacy Information Center), 'Former Secrets: Documents Released Under the FOIA', 1998.

Escobar, Arturo, and Sonia E. Alvarez (eds), *The Making of Social Movements in Latin America: Identity, Strategy and Democracy*, Boulder, CO, Westview Press, 1992.

Far Eastern Economic Review, 'Internet TV: Ready for Action', 1 June 2000.

Feenberg, Andrew, *Critical Theory of Technology*, New York, Oxford University Press, 1991.

Flakoll A, Erick, 'Democracia cibernética', *Pensamiento Propio*, no. 105, August 1993, pp. 17–24.

Fortier, François, 'Living with Cyberspace: Vietnam's Latest Dilemma', pp. 237–45 in Dan Duffy (ed.), *North Viet Nam Now: Fiction and Essays from Ha Noi* (Viet Nam Forum 15), New Haven, CT, Yale University Press, 1996.

Fortier, François, *Civil Society Computer Networks: The Perilous Road of Cyber-Politics*, Ph.D. dissertation, Toronto, York University, 1997.

Fortier, François, 'Virtual Communities, Real Struggles: Seeking Alternatives for Democratic Networking', pp. 446–69 in Michael Gurstein (ed.), *Community Informatics: Enabling Communities with Information and Communications Technologies*, Hershey, PA, and London, Idea Group Publishing, 2000.

Frederick, Howard H., 'Breaking the Global Information Blockade Using the Technologies of Peace and War', Conference on Computers for Social Change: Tools for Progressive Action, Hunter College, New York, 26 June 1991.

Frederick, Howard H., *Global Communication and International Relations*, Belmont, CA, Wadsworth, 1993.

Friedman, Thomas, *The Lexus and the Olive Tree*, London, HarperCollins, 1999.

Ghazanfar, S.M., 'Third World Technological Change: Some

Perspectives on Socio-economic Implications', *The Journal of Social, Political and Economic Studies*, vol. 15, no. 1, Spring 1990, pp. 91–105.

Gillespie, Andrew and Kevin Robins, 'Geographical Inequalities: The Spatial Bias of the New Communications Technologies', *Journal of Communication*, vol. 39, no. 3, Summer 1989, pp. 7–18.

Girard, Bruce (ed.), *A Passion for Radio*, Montreal, Black Rose Books, 1992.

GLAAD (Gay and Lesbian Alliance Against Defamation), *Access Denied: An Impact of Internet Filtering Software on the Gay and Lesbian Community*, 1997, http://www.glaad.org/glaad/access_denied/.

Golding, Peter, 'World Wide Wedge: Division and Contradiction in the Global Information Infrastructure', *Monthly Review*, vol. 48, no. 3, July–August 1996, pp. 70–85.

Gordon, Robert, 'Not Much of a New Economy', *Financial Times*, 26 July 2000.

Greenberg, Lawrence T., and Seymour E. Goodman, 'Is Big Brother Hanging by His Bootstraps?', *Communications of the ACM*, vol. 39, no. 7, July 1996, pp. 11–15.

Gurstein, Michael, 'Information and Communications Technology and Local Economic Development: Towards a New Local Economy', in Gertrude Ann MacIntyre (ed.), *Perspectives on Communities*, Sydney, Nova Scotia, UCCB Press, 1998.

Hamelink, Cees, 'New Information and Communication Technologies: Social Development and Cultural Change', Geneva, United Nations Research Institute for Social Development, Discussion Paper no. 86, 1997.

Harding, James, 'Top of the Ratings', *Financial Times*, 16 December 1999.

Heeks, Richard, 'Information and Communication Technologies, Poverty and Development', Institute for Development Policy and

Management, University of Manchester, Development Informatics Working Paper Series, Working Paper No. 5, 1999.

Herman, Edward S., 'The Propaganda Model Revisited', *Monthly Review*, vol. 48, no. 3, July–August 1996, pp. 115–28.

Hills, Jill, 'The Telecommunication Rich and Poor', *Third World Quarterly*, vol. 12, no. 2, April 1990, pp. 71–90.

Hirschkop, Ken, 'Democracy and the New Technologies', *Monthly Review*, vol. 48, no. 3, July-August 1996, pp. 86–98.

Huyer, Sophia, 'Supporting Women's Use of Information Technologies for Sustainable Development', Ottawa. Submitted to the Gender and Sustainable Development Unit, IDRC, 18 February 1997.

Inoue, Cristina, 'Organizações Não-governamentais e Redes de Comunicação', MA Thesis in International Relations, Universidade de Brasília, 1995, http://www.marujo.com/carel/.

Jackson, Tim, 'Strong Brands Stand Tall in On-line Shake-out', *Financial Times*, 21 March 2000.

Jackson, Tony, 'Safeguard Your Skills from the Cherry-pickers', *Connectis*, Issue 1, 1999.

Karelse, Cathy-Mae, 'Reconceptualising Education for the Production, Use and Management of ICTs', IDRC contribution to UNECA International Conference on African Women and Economic Development, 1998.

Kauffmann, Sylvie,'Le cybercitoyen modèle est mâle, blanc, jeune et américain', *Le Monde (Supplément Multimédia)*, 30 September 1996.

Kehoe, Louise, 'Inside Track: AppleSoup's recipe for revenue: A breakaway from Napster's music website aims to make file-swapping a profitable enterprise', *Financial Times*, 20 July 2000.

Kline, David, 'The Myth of Disintermediation', *Market Forces*, 1996.

Kole, Ellen S., 'Whose Empowerment? NGOs Between Grassroots and Netizens', Working paper available at http://dkglobal.org/crit-ict, 1998.

Kole, Ellen S., 'Myths and Realities in Internet Discourse: Using Computer Networks for Data Collection and the Beijing World Conference on Women', *Gazette: The International Journal for Communication Studies*, vol. 60, no. 4, August 1998, pp. 343–60.

Konrad, Rachel, 'Net Consolidation as a Natural, Accelerated Business Cycle', *CNET News.com*, 23 June 2000.

Lamprière, Luc, 'Microsoft s'attaque au téléspectateur américain', *Libération*, 14 January 1998.

Lebovich, Mark, 'At Amazon.com, It's a Jungle: The New Economy Needs Speed', *International Herald Tribune*, 23 November 1999.

Lee, Eric, *The Labour Movement and the Internet: The New Internationalism*, London, Pluto Press, 1997.

Leiner, Barry, *et al.*, 'A Brief History of the Internet', *Internet Society*, 1997, http://www.isoc.org/internet/history/.

Lemos, Rob, 'Will China Squash Hong Kong's Net Freedoms?', *ZDNet*, 30 June 1997.

Lewis, Peter H., 'On-line Service Cracks Down on Junk E-mail', *International Herald Tribune*, 6 September 1996, p. 14.

Lipnack, Jessica and Jeffrey Stamps, *The Network Book: People Connecting With People*, New York, Routledge & Kegan Paul, 1986.

McAnany, Emile G., Jorge Schnitman and Noreene Janus (eds), *Communication and Social Structure: Critical Studies in Mass Media Research*, New York, Praeger, 1981.

McChesney, Robert W., 'The Political Economy of Global Communication', pp. 1–26 in Robert W. McChesney, Ellen Meiksins Wood and John Bellamy Foster, *Capitalism and the Information Age: The Political Economy of the Global Communication Revolution*, New York, Monthly Review Press, 1998.

McChesney, Robert W., Ellen Meiksins Wood and John Bellamy Foster, *Capitalism and the Information Age: The Political Economy of the Global Communication Revolution*, New York, Monthly Review Press, 1998.

McCullagh, Declan, 'U.S. Wants to Trace Net Users', *Wired*, 4 March 2000.

Mackintosh, James, 'Customers to Benefit from Internet's Explosive Impact', *Financial Times*, 1 December 1999, p. IV.

Madson, Wayne, 'Cryptography and Liberty: An International Survey of Encryption Policy', GILC (Global Internet Liberty Campaign), 1997.

Manchester, Philip, 'Network Devices Challenge PC', *Financial Times*, 1 December 1999, p. IT-V.

Martin, Michèle, *Communication and Social Forms: A Study of the Development of the Telephone System, 1876–1920*, Ph.D. dissertation, University of Toronto, 1987.

Meiksins Wood, Ellen, 'The Uses and Abuses of Civil Society', pp. 60–84 in Ralph Miliband, Leo Panitch and John Saville (eds), *Socialist Register 1990*, London, Merlin Press, 1990.

Meiksins Wood, Ellen, 'Labor, the State, and Class Struggle', *Monthly Review*, vol. 49, no. 3, July–August 1997, pp. 1–17.

Meiksins Wood, Ellen, 'Modernity, Postmodernity, or Capitalism?', pp. 27–49 in Robert W. McChesney, Ellen Meiksins Wood and John Bellamy Foster, *Capitalism and the Information Age: The Political Economy of the Global Communication Revolution*, New York, Monthly Review Press, 1998.

Melody, William H, 'La négociation des termes du transfert technologique en communication', *Revue Tiers Monde*, vol. 28, no. 111, July–September 1987, pp. 701–7.

Menzies, Heather, *Whose Brave New World? The Information Highway and the New Economy*, Toronto, Between the Lines, 1996.

Morin, Hervé, 'Le diamètre de la Toile est revu à la hausse', *Le Monde*, 2 June 2000, p. 21.

Mosco, Vincent, 'Computers and Democracy', pp. 215–31 in Jacques

Berleur *et al.* (eds), *The Information Society: Evolving Landscapes*, New York, Springer-Verlag and Captus University Publishers, 1990.

Mosco, Vincent, *The Political Economy of Communication: Rethinking and Renewal*, London, Sage, 1996.

Mosco, Vincent, 'Political Economy, Communication, and Labor', pp. 13–38 in Gerald Sussman and John A. Lent (eds), *Global Productions: Labor in the Making of the 'Information Society'*, Cresskill, NJ, Hampton Press, 1998.

Mosco, Vincent and Andrew Herman, 'Radical Social Theory and the Communications Revolution', pp. 58–84 in Emile G. McAnany, Jorge Schnitman and Noreene Janus (eds), *Communication and Social Structure: Critical Studies in Mass Media Research*, New York, Praeger, 1981.

Mosco, Vincent and Janet Wasko (eds), *The Political Economy of Information*, Madison, University of Wisconsin Press, 1988.

Munyua, Hilda, 'Application of Information Communication Technologies in the Agricultural Sector in Africa: A Gender Perspective with Special Reference to Women'. Paper presented at the United Nations Economic Commission for Africa (UNECA) International Conference on African Women and Economic Development, 1998.

Negroponte, Nicholas, *Being Digital*, London, Coronet, 1995.

Neumann, Peter G., 'Risks on the Information Superhighway', *Communications of the ACM*, vol. 37, no. 6, June 1994, p. 114.

Noble, David F., *America by Design: Science, Technology, and the Rise of Corporate Capitalism*, New York, Alfred A. Knopf, 1977.

Noble, David F., *Forces of Production: A Social History of Industrial Automation*, New York, Alfred A. Knopf, 1984.

Noble, David F., *Progress Without People: New Technologies, Unemployment, and the Message of Resistance*, Toronto, Between the Lines, 1995.

OECD (Organization for Economic Co-operation and Development),

'OECD Adopts Guidelines For Cryptography Policy', News Release, 27 March 1997.

Ogden, Michael R., 'Politics in a Parallel Universe: Is There a Future for Cyberdemocracy?', *Futures* (London), vol. 26, no. 7, September 1994, pp. 713–29.

PoKempner, Dinah, 'Encryption in the Service of Human Rights', Briefing Paper, Human Rights Watch, 1 August 1997.

Press, Larry, 'Will Commercial Networks Prevail in Emerging Nations?', *OnTheInternet*, March–April 1997, pp. 40–41.

Raymond, Eric S., 'Homesteading the Noosphere', April 1998, http://www.tuxedo.org/~esr/writings/homesteading.

Renault, Enguérand, 'Fidéliser le client est désormais plus important que détenir la dernière technologie', and 'La bataille pour la troisième génération de téléphone mobile commence', *Le Monde*, 29 February 2000, p. 23.

Reporter Sans Frontière, Communiqué de presse, 'Les vingt ennemis d'Internet', 9 August 1999.

Rheingold, Howard, *The Virtual Community: Homesteading on the Electronic Frontier*, Reading, Addison-Wesley, 1993.

Rheingold, Howard, *The Virtual Community: Finding Connection in a Computerized World*, London, Secker & Warburg, 1994.

Richardson, Don, 'The Internet and Rural Development: Recommendations for Strategy and Activity', *SD Dimensions* (FAO), August 1996.

Robins, Kevin and Frank Webster, 'Cybernetic Capitalism: Information, Technology, Everyday Life', pp. 44–75 in Vincent Mosco and Janet Wasko (eds), *The Political Economy of Information*, Madison, University of Wisconsin Press, 1988.

Rohozinski, Rafal, 'Mapping Russian Cyberspace: Perspective on Democracy and the Net'. Paper presented at the UNRISD Conference on Information Technologies and Social Development, Geneva, 22–24 June 1998.

Roszak, Theodore, 'Dumbing Us Down', *New Internationalist*, Issue 286, December 1996.

Sagawa, Paul, 'The Balkanization of the Internet', *McKinsey Quarterly*, no. 1, 1997, pp. 127–37.

Salvaggio, Jerry L. (ed.), *Telecommunications: Issues and Choices for Society*, New York, Longman, 1983.

Sandoval, Greg, 'Failed Dot-coms May Be Selling Your Private Information', *CNET News.com*, 29 June 2000.

Sardar, Ziauddin and Jerome R. Ravetz (eds), *Cyberfutures: Culture and Politics on the Information Superhighway*, London, Pluto Press, 1996.

Schiller, Herbert I., *Information and the Crisis Economy*, Norwood, NJ, Ablex, 1984.

Schiller, Herbert I., 'La communication, une affaire d'État pour Washington', *Manière de Voir, Le Monde Diplomatique*, no. 46, July–August 1999, pp. 65–8.

Schuler, Douglas, *New Community Networks: Wired for Change*, Reading, Addison-Wesley, 1996.

Sédallian, Valérie, 'Controlling illegal content over the Internet: the French situation'. Paper presented at 'Censoring the Internet: a lawyer's deceit', Media Law Committee, 26th International Bar Association Conference, Berlin, 23 October 1996.

Sédallian, Valérie, 'Cryptographie: les enjeux et l'état de la législation française', *L'Internet Juridique*, 1997.

Shiva, Vandana, 'The Politics of the Green Revolution', *Third World Resurgence*, no. 33, May 1993, pp. 4–8.

Spencer, George, 'Microcybernetics as the Meta-Technology of Pure Control', in Ziauddin Sardar and Jerome R. Ravetz, *Cyberfutures: Culture and Politics on the Information Superhighway*, London, Pluto Press, 1996, pp. 61–89.

Stallabrass, Julian, 'Empowering Technology: The Exploration of Cyberspace', *New Left Review*, 211, May–June 1995, pp. 3–32.

Stewart, Frances, *Technology and Underdevelopment*, London, Macmillan, 1978.

Sussman, Gerald, *The Political Economy of Telecommunication Transfer: Transnationalizing the New Philippines Information Order*, Ph.D. dissertation, University of Hawaii, 1983.

Sussman, Gerald, *Communication, Technology, and Politics in the Information Age*, Thousand Oaks, CA, Sage, 1997.

Sussman , Gerald and John A. Lent (eds), *Global Productions: Labor in the Making of the 'information society'*, Cresskill, NJ, Hampton Press, 1998.

Swett, Charles, *Strategic Assessment: The Internet*, Washington, 17 July 1995, Office of the Assistant Secretary of Defense for Special Operations and Low-Intensity Conflict (Policy Planning), Pentagon, http://www.fas.org/.

Taylor, Marcus, 'Servicing the Wireless Internet Market', *Zum Thema*, no. 38, 3 March 2000.

Tester, Keith, *Civil Society*, London, Routledge, 1992.

The Economist, 'Liberty.com', 30 October 1999.

The Economist, 'Electronic Commerce: Amazon's Delta', 20 November 1999.

The Economist, 'Frictions in Cyberspace: Retailing on the Internet, it is said, is almost Perfectly Competitive. Really?', 20 November 1999.

The Economist, 'Readjusting the Lens', 20 November 1999.

The Economist, 'Citizens' Groups: The Nongovernmental Order', 11 December 1999.

The Economist, 'The Fright After Christmas', 5 February 2000.

The Economist, 'Reuters Setting Up Shop', 12 February 2000.

The Economist, 'Dotty about dot.commerce?', 26 February 2000.

The Economist, 'Shopping Around the Web', 26 February 2000.

The Economist, 'Seller Beware', 4 March 2000.

The Economist, 'The Internet: Can You?', 10 March 2000.

The Economist, 'The Consensus Machine', 10 June 2000.

The Economist, 'Electronic Surveillance: Being Watched', 26 August 2000.

The Economist, 'AOL's Cautious Privacy Stance', 22 January 2000.

Thoumyre, Lionel, *Abuses in the Cyberspace: The Regulation of Illicit Messages Diffused on the Internet*, Master of Arts, ESST, Université Louis Pasteur, Strasbourg, Faculté Notre Dame de la Paix, CRID, Namur, 1996.

Underhill, G.R.D., 'Conceptualizing the Changing Global Order', pp. 17–44 in R. Stubbs and G.R.D. Underhill (eds), *Political Economy and the Changing Global Order*, London, Macmillan, 1994.

UNESCO, *Information and Communication Technologies in Development: A UNESCO Perspective*, Paris, UNESCO Secretariat, 1996.

Valloppillil, Vinod, 'Open Source Software: A (New?) Development Methodology', Leaked Internal Microsoft document, 11 August 1998.

van Koert, Robin, 'Bustling and Sprawling Cities: A Natural Environment for ICTs'. Working paper available at http://dkglobal.org/crit-ict, 1998.

Vasconi, Cristina, 'Más que un teléfono: ¿Qué ventajas nos ofrecen las telecomunicaciones?', *Pensamiento Propio*, no. 105, August 1993, pp. 21–2.

Verzola, Roberto, 'Globalization: The Third Wave'. Paper presented at 'Colonialism to Globalization: Five Centuries After Vasco da Gama', New Delhi, 5 February 1998, http:/www.dkglobal.org/.

Walker, Christopher, 'Orthodox Jews Go Surfing on the Kosher Internet', *The Times* (London), 21 October 1996, p. 12.

Warren, Michael H., 'Implementation of the Communications Assistance for Law Enforcement Act (CALEA)', Washington, 23 October 1997, Statement Before the Subcommittee on Crime, Committee on the Judiciary, United States House of Representatives, http://www.fbi.gov/.

Whitaker, Reg, 'The Tower of Infobabel: Cyberspace as Alternative Universe', pp. 173–88 in Leo Panitch (ed.), *Socialist Register 1996: Are There Alternatives?*, London, Merlin Press, 1996.

Wingfield, Nick and Glenn R. Simpson, 'AOL's Cautious Privacy Stance', *The Wall Street Journal Europe*, 16 March 2000.

Winner, Langdon, *The Whale and the Reactor: A Search for Limits in an Age of High Technology*, Chicago and London, University of Chicago Press, 1986.